Fingering Mastery

scales & modes for the bass fingerboard

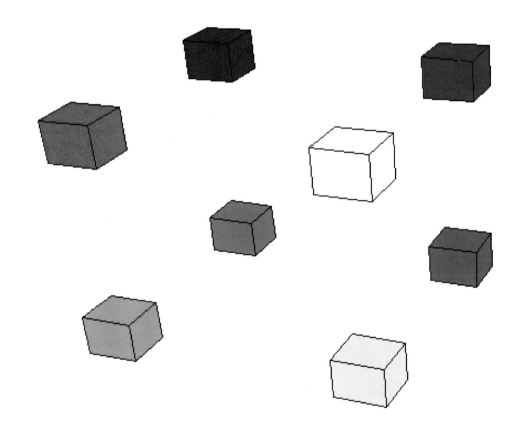

by Jeff Brent and Schell Barkley

Fingering Mastery
scales & modes for the bass fingerboard

Dogbite Music Publications
Copyright © 2012
by Jeff Brent and Schell Barkley

ISBN-10: 1477463860
ISBN-13: 978-1477463864

www.FingeringMastery.com

Fingering Mastery
scales & modes for the bass fingerboard

Preface

This is a study guide for those who wish to further their understanding of bass scale fingerings in an intelligent, and orderly manner.

The principles of radial symmetry in music and the interlocking relationships of the chromatic cube make it possible to map out on the fretboard all the essential western scales in easy-to-remember patterns that are perfectly logical, and, most importantly, 100% practical for ease of execution in performance.

Among the many innovations in this handbook is the descriptive use of color throughout. This enables the player to most clearly and graphically visualize the differences *and* similarities between related scales.

The study begins with the 7-note scales: first the Ionian and its modes, then the harmonic minor, followed by the jazz minor and Harmonic Major - displayed in cohesive full-color patterns which promote both memorization and ease of fingering.

Next, the Chromatic Cube section revisits the Ionian & jazz minor sets, and introduces the Wholetone scale, the diminisheds and Bebop Major set fingerings - all examined in great detail.

And finally, an investigation into the pentatonics leads to the inclusion of the octatonic Bebop Dominant set.

A quick flip-through of these pages will make it obvious to bassists of any level that the simple graphic exposition of fretboard systems presented in this book really *IS* a better mousetrap.

It's the only bass scale fingering book you'll ever need

Table of Contents

Dedicated to Randa Lee

Intro

The diatonic major scale and its modes are perhaps the most important tools for study and performance, along with the pentatonic and blues scales.

These are shown in various configurations designed to highlight the intervallic relationships and repetition of fragments between groups of strings.

On pages 5, 41, 47 and 53 are found respectively the 5-Box bass fingerings for the Ionian and its modes, the harmonic minor, jazz minor set, and Harmonic Major scales.

These visualizations yield compact and comfortable hand positions with a minimum of memorization (only five boxes per scale).

When examining any of those four scales in depth, its 5-Box fingering is a great place to begin your quest.

In the chapter on the "7-Box sets" (pgs 6-37), the Ionian family modes are analyzed in detail.

This fingering system is based on the two minor tetrachords in the A natural minor heptatonic scale juxtaposed parallel to each other on the fingerboard:

D E F G
A B C **D**

Adding another set of parallel minor tetrachord pairs an octave away to the fretboard layout creates logical (ie. easily memorable) interlocking boxes.

| D E F | G
| A B C | D
D | E F G |
A | B C D |

In this system, there is never a span greater than three frets. This ensures maximum fingering comfort while still making it possibile to rip through two octaves of the major scale and its modes with the greatest of ease.

Also noteworthy is how the both the larger systems presented in the "7-Box" Ionian set study overlap and conjoin with one another. Gaining a thorough facility at transitioning between these two main fingering regions is a giant step towards total command of these ubiquituous scales and modes.

The "9-Box" systems (pgs 42-45 [hm], 48-51 [jm], 54-57 [HM]) are an efficient way to picture these three related scales as adjacent 2-string and 3-string patterns.

Begin by conquering these two- and three-string boxes, then move back-and-forth between them, expanding to incorporate all four strings into your practice routine.

The crown jewel of this bassist's handbook is the 12-page chapter on the Chromatic Cube Bass Fingerings (pgs 62-73).

The Cube is a representation of major scales, jazz minor scales, diminished scales, the wholetone scale, and the bebop major scale.

In other words, all the essential and most common scales in occidental musics.

The Chromatic Cube section illustrates how intimately all these structures are related and how to mutate one scale into a neighboring scale via simple alteration. Combined alterations result in atonal scales (diminished, wholetone).

Practice suggestion: <u>Work one Cube per month</u>. Fix in your mind and fingers the similarities and differences between the related scales and their relative degrees. In the space of one short year you'll have internalized them all. Time well spent!

The primordial pentatonics (pgs 74-75) are perhaps the most common melodic structures explored by advancing players. Although only a scant two pages are devoted to them here, all the most useful and relevant boxes are included.

An interesting thing occurs when we combine the two major and minor pentatonic scales with the same root (pgs 76-79):

C major pentatonic
C D E G A

C minor pentatonic
C E♭ F G B♭

The octatonic scale generated by this combination of the C pentatonics is the fifth mode of the F Bebop Dominant Scale (aka *Mixodorian, Mixolydian add ♭3, Dorian add 3, Bebop dorian, Bebop minor,* etc).

Compare:

Combined C major and C minor pentatonics
(Mixo-Dorian hybrid)

C D E♭ E F G A B♭ C

1 2 ♭3 3 4 5 6 ♭7 8

F Bebop Dominant Scale

F G A B♭ C D E♭ E F

1 2 3 4 5 6 ♭7 7 8

Enjoy the journey!

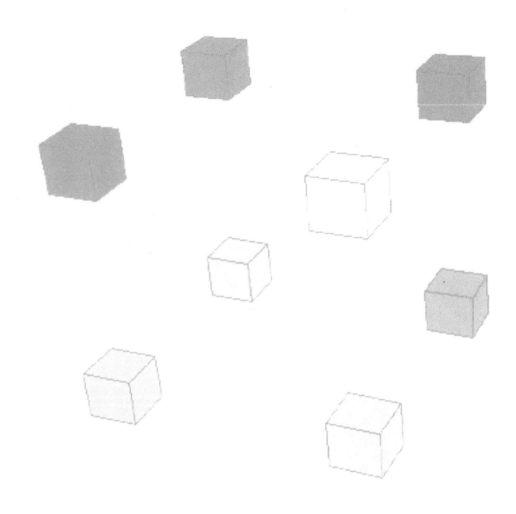

Ionian: 5-box set

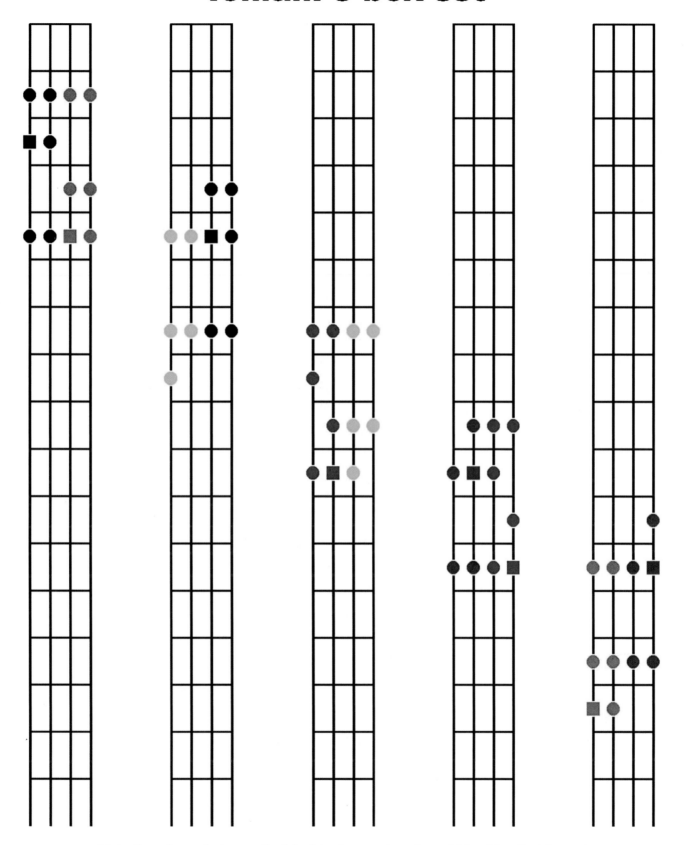

Note the mirrors between the black/red, green/purple and blue/blue 2-string sets.

The "7-Box" Sets System for Fingering the Diatonic Modes

Due to the unique radial symmetry of the Aeolian mode (aka "natural minor"), it is possible to position all seven notes of the major scale on any two strings of the bass using parallel minor tetrachords.

For the following examples and explanations,
the notes A B C D E F G were chosen.

On string 4, we have the minor tetrachord composed of A B C D.
On string 3, we have the minor tetrachord D E F G.

In figure 1.01 below, "A" is located on string 4 fret 5, "B" is on string 4 fret 7, "C" is on string 4 fret 8. "D" is located both on string 4 fret 10 AND on string 3 fret 5.
"E" is on string 3 fret 7, "F" on string 3 fret 8 and "G" is on string 3 fret 10.

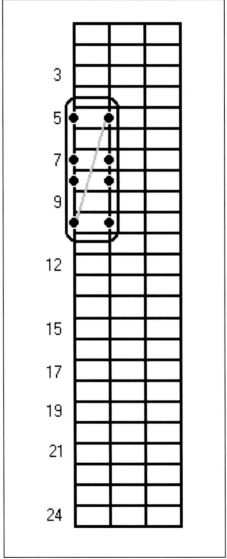

figure 1.01

Due to the scale of the bass, it generally proves inconvenient to play tetrachords as a four-finger position.

The advantage to organizing notes in two parallel minor tetrachords is that it gives the bassist the option of using TWO positions, each of which is a comfortable spread of only three frets.

In figure 1.02, we have a position that covers the notes A B C D E F using the index finger on fret 5 of either string, the ring finger on frets 7 and the pinky finger on fret 8 of either string. In figure 1.03, we have a position that covers the notes B C D E F G using the index finger on frets 7, the middle finger on frets 8 and the pinky finger on frets 10.

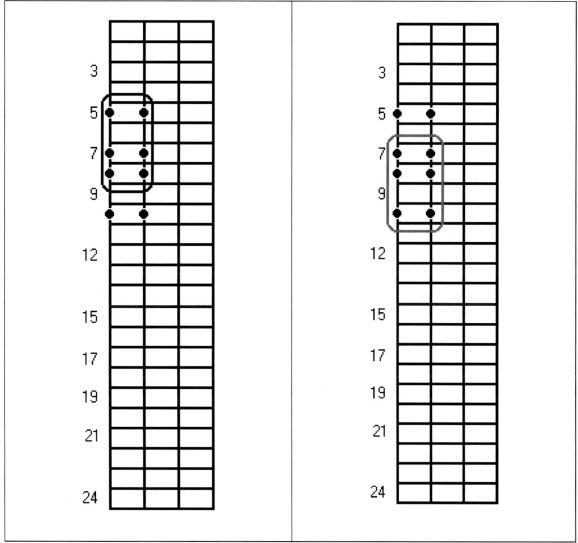

figure 1.02   figure 1.03

To move back and forth between these two positions is a simple matter: When going from the lower position (black box) up to the higher position (red box), slide the pinky finger from fret 8 to fret 10. When moving from the upper position (red box) down to the lower position (black box), slide the index finger from fret 7 to fret 5.

Box Set #1: The Red Box

In figure 1.04, a second set of parallel minor tetrachords is added. This set is identical to the one presented in the introduction on strings 5 and 6, except that it is one octave higher.

With the addition of this new parallel tetrachord set on strings 1 and 2, it is possible to construct a box with a spread of three frets that spans the four strings (figure 1.05).

The index finger falls on fret 7 throughout as does the pinky finger on fret 10.
The middle finger is on frets 8 on strings 3 & 4, and on strings 1 & 2 the ring finger falls on fret 9.

This provides an easy and comfortable way to navigate an octave and a half of the scale.

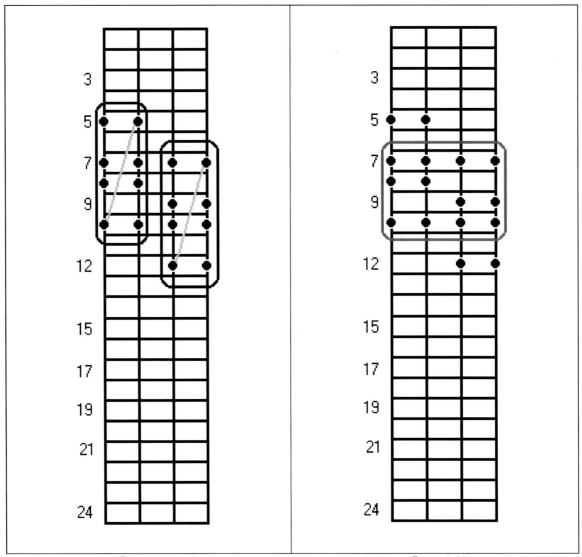

figure 1.04   figure 1.05

In figure 1.06 we combine the red box with an auxiliary lower extension represented by the black box.

As described earlier, it is a simple matter to transition between these two boxes by either sliding the index finger down a whole step to move from the red box to the black box or by sliding up a whole step with the pinky finger to move from the black box into the red box.

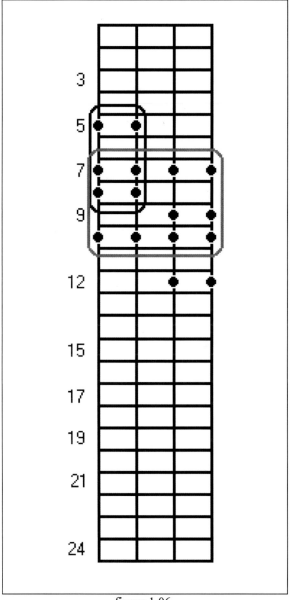

figure 1.06

Box Set #1: Complete

As can be clearly seen from figure 1.07, "Box Set #1" consists of one main box (the red box) with auxiliary lower and upper extensions (represented respectively by the black box and the purple box).

The fingering transitions between the red box & the black box have been covered previously.

To effect the transition from the red box up to the purple box (as you have surely already guessed), move the pinky finger up two frets (a whole step) from 10th fret to 12th fret.

Moving from the purple box down to the red box is done by simply sliding the index finger down from 9th fret to 7th fret.

This allows the bassist to easily navigate almost two full octaves using comfortable fingering based on extremely simple and consistent logic.

Box Set #1: Complete

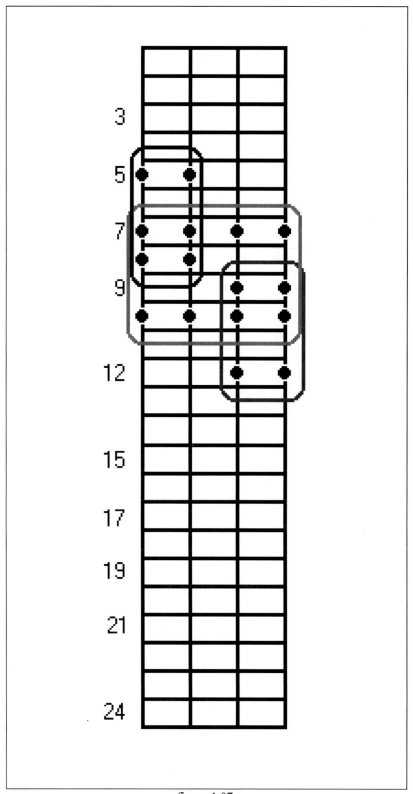

figure 1.07

Box Set #1: The Aeolian Mode

(aka "the natural minor scale")

Figures 1.08 and 1.09 below show the placement of the roots of Aeolian mode.

The Aeolian roots are indicated by the aqua colored dots.

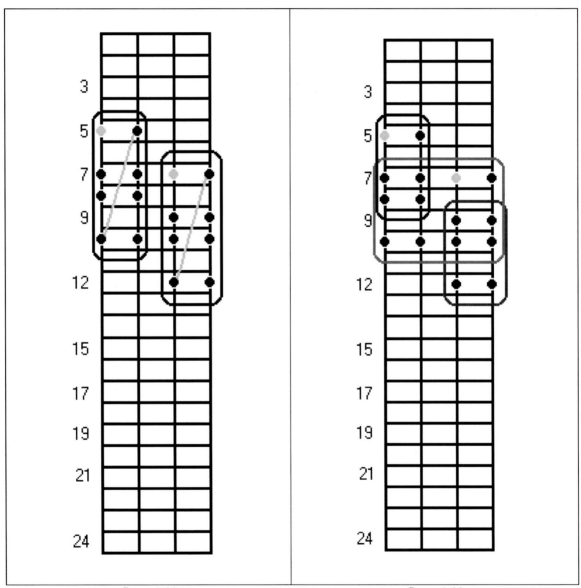

figure 1.08   figure 1.09

Box Set #1: The Ionian Mode
(aka "The Major Scale")

Figures 1.10 and 1.11 below show the placement of the roots of Ionian mode.

The Ionian roots are indicated by the green colored dots.

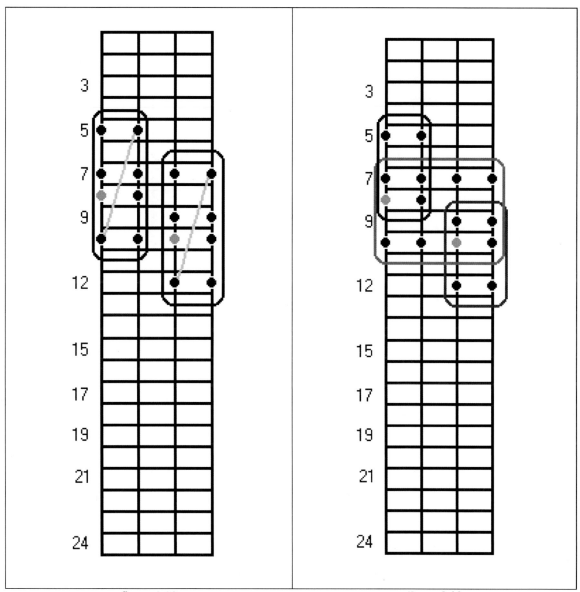

figure 1.10   figure 1.11

Box Set #1: The Dorian Mode

Figures 1.12 and 1.13 below show the placement of the roots of Dorian mode.

The Dorian roots are indicated by the brown colored dots.

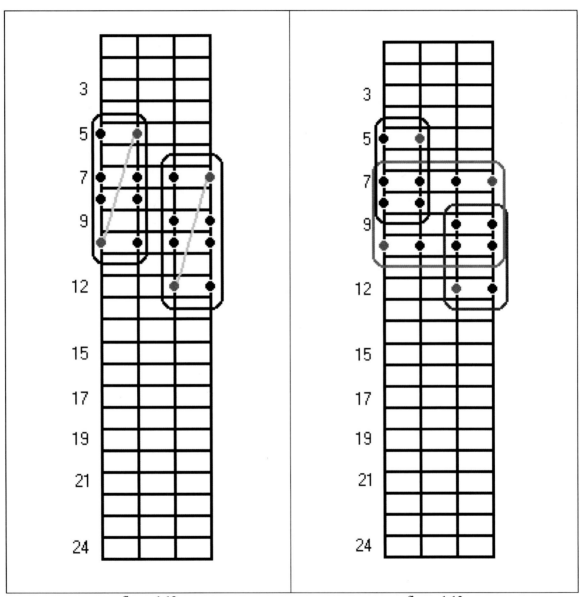

figure 1.12   figure 1.13

Box Set #1: The Phrygian Mode
(aka "Spanish minor")

Figures 1.14 and 1.15 below show the placement of the roots of Phrygian mode.

The Phrygian roots are indicated by the red colored dots.

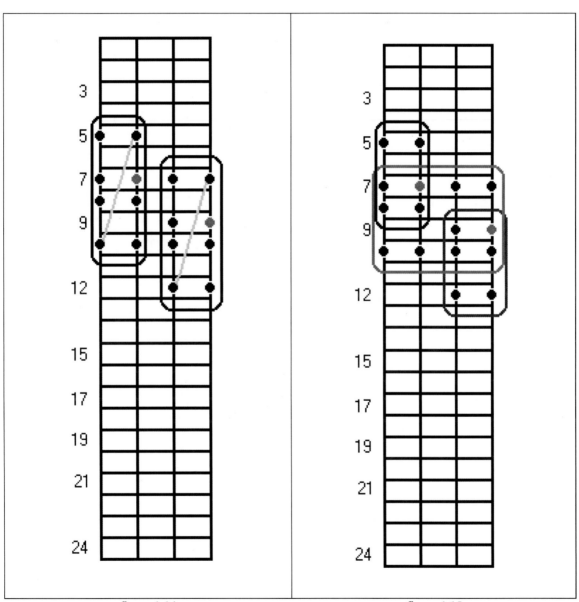

figure 1.14   figure 1.15

Box Set #1: The Lydian Mode

Figures 1.16 and 1.17 below show the placement of the roots of Lydian mode.

The Lydian roots are indicated by the purple colored dots.

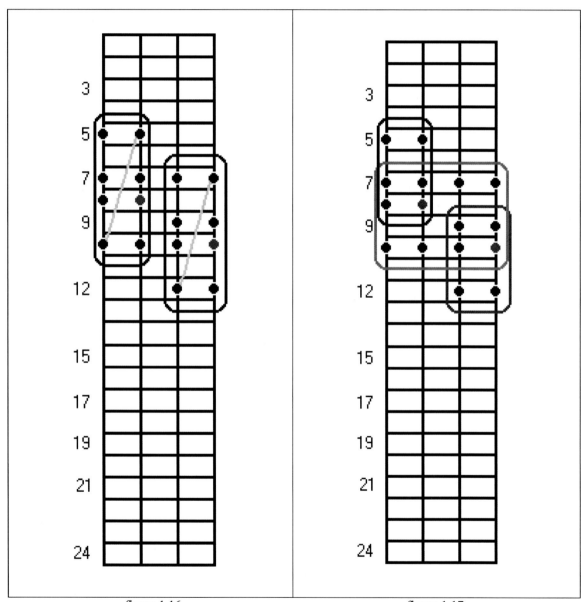

figure 1.16   figure 1.17

Box Set #1: The Mixolydian Mode

Figures 1.18 and 1.19 below show the placement of the roots of Mixolydian mode.

The Mixolydian roots are indicated by the orange colored dots.

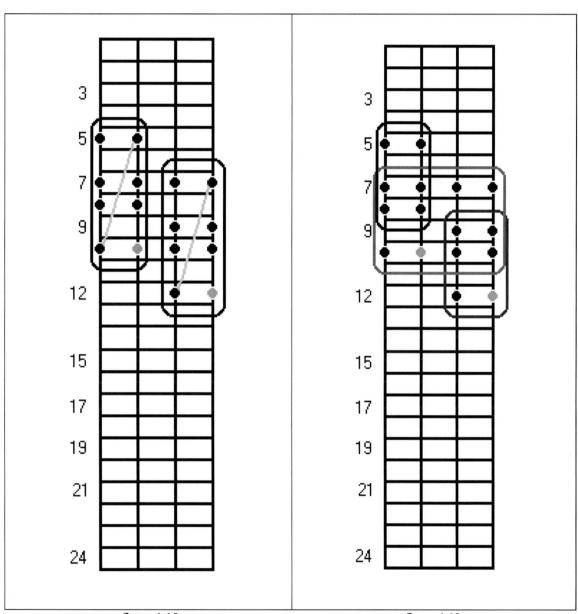

figure 1.18   figure 1.19

Box Set #1: The Locrian Mode

Figures 1.20 and 1.21 below show the placement of the roots of Locrian mode.

The Locrian roots are indicated by the yellow colored dots.

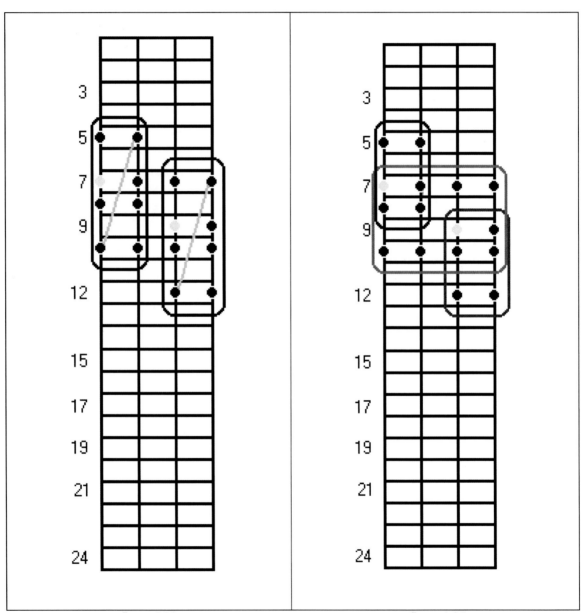

figure 1.20   figure 1.21

Box Set #1: All Mode Roots

Figures 1.22 and 1.23 below show the placement of the roots of all seven modes.
Aeolian Roots = Aqua
Locrian Roots = Yellow
Ionian Roots = Green
Dorian Roots = Brown
Phrygian Roots = Red
Lydian Roots = Purple
Mixolydian Roots = Orange

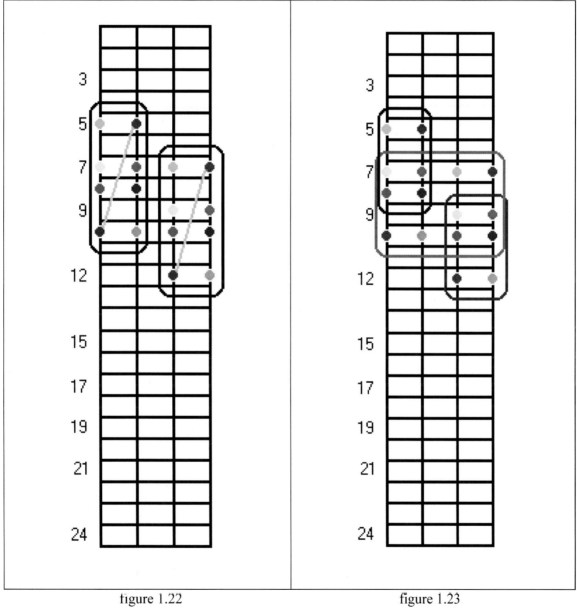

figure 1.22   figure 1.23

Another convenient feature to this system is that if you're looking for the next note "outside the box", it is always a whole step (2 frets) immediately above the highest note in your current box or likewise a whole step immediately below the lowest note in that box.

These outside "safe notes" are represented as open circles in figure 1.24 below.

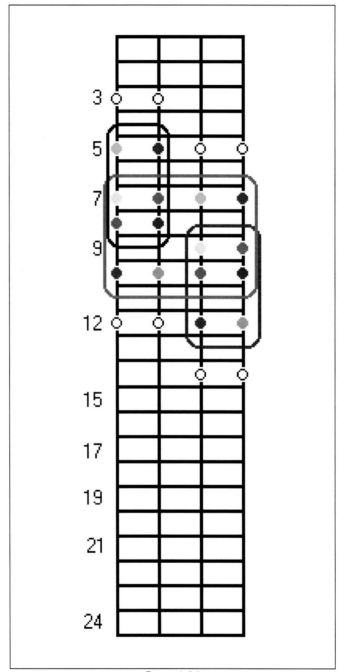

figure 1.24

Box Set #1
with outside "safe" notes

Box Set #2: Complete

Figure 2.01 below illustrates the placement of the parallel minor tetrachord pair on strings 2 & 3, along with the minor tetrachord built off the 2nd degree of the major scale on string 4 and the minor tetrachord built off the 6th degree of the major scale on string 1.

Figure 2.02 shows the two boxes of this set (brown and green) which span three strings apiece covering almost two octaves.

Note that this configuration leaves two "orphans" outside of "Box Set #2" which are located (in this instance) on string 4 fret 10 and string 1 fret 19.

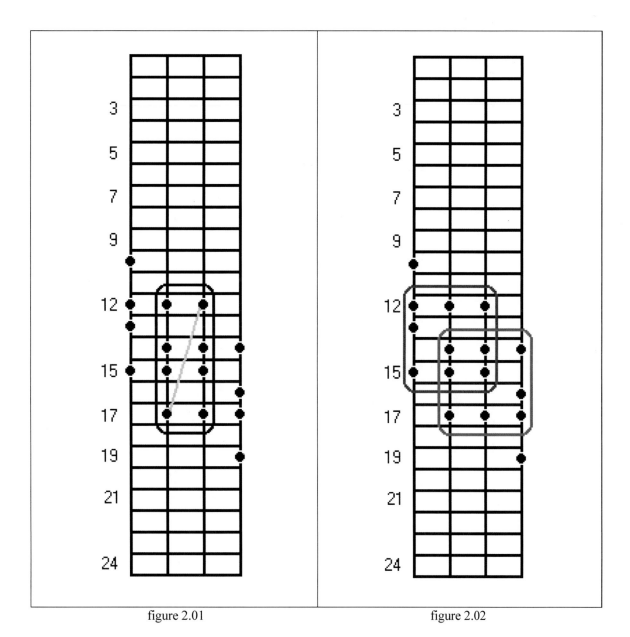

figure 2.01   figure 2.02

Box Set #2

Box Set #2: The Aeolian Mode
(aka "the natural minor scale")

Figures 2.03 and 2.04 below show the placement of the roots of Aeolian mode.

The Aeolian roots are indicated by the aqua colored dots.

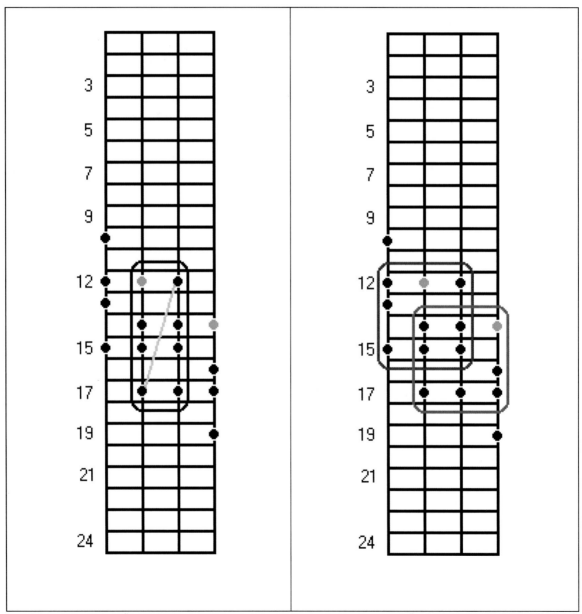

figure 2.03   figure 2.04

Box Set #2: The Ionian Mode
(aka "The Major Scale")

Figures 2.05 and 2.06 below show the placement of the roots of Ionian mode.

The Ionian roots are indicated by the green colored dots.

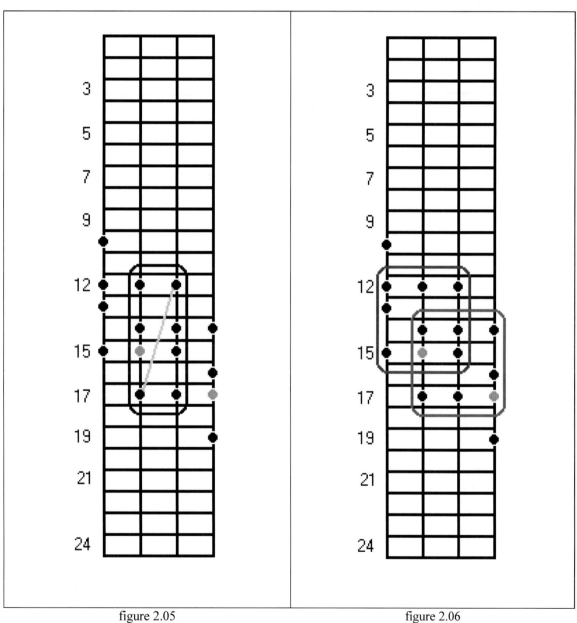

figure 2.05   figure 2.06

Box Set #2: The Dorian Mode

Figures 2.07 and 2.08 below show the placement of the roots of Dorian mode.

The Dorian roots are indicated by the brown colored dots.

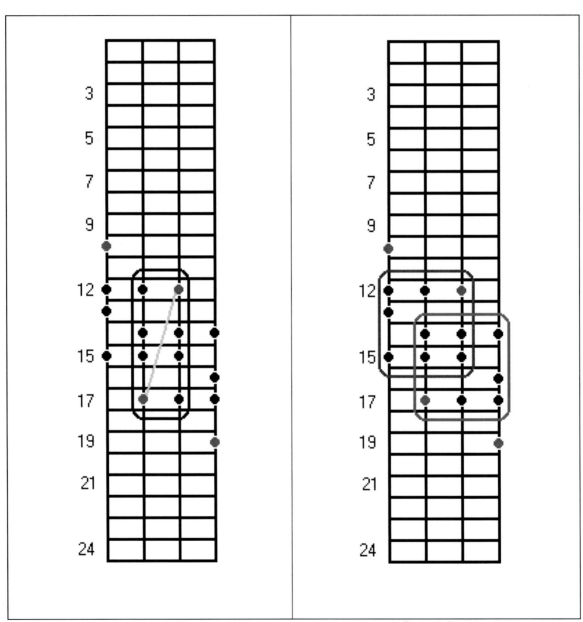

figure 2.07   figure 2.08

Box Set #2: The Phrygian Mode
(aka "Spanish minor")

Figures 2.09 and 2.10 below show the placement of the roots of Phrygian mode.

The Phrygian roots are indicated by the red colored dots.

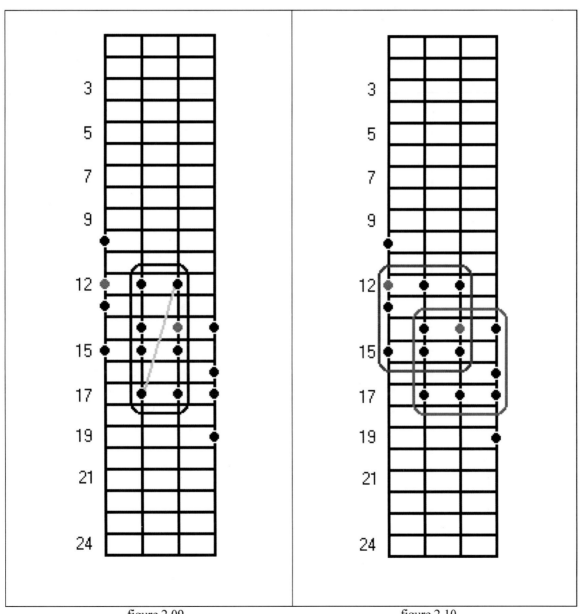

figure 2.09   figure 2.10

Box Set #2: The Lydian Mode

Figures 2.11 and 2.12 below show the placement of the roots of Lydian mode.

The Lydian roots are indicated by the purple colored dots.

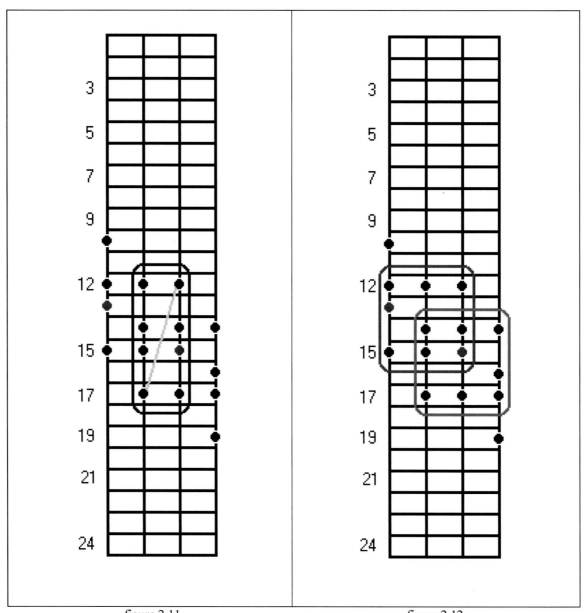

figure 2.11   figure 2.12

Box Set #2: The Mixolydian Mode

Figures 2.13 and 2.14 below show the placement of the roots of Mixolydian mode.

The Mixolydian roots are indicated by the orange colored dots.

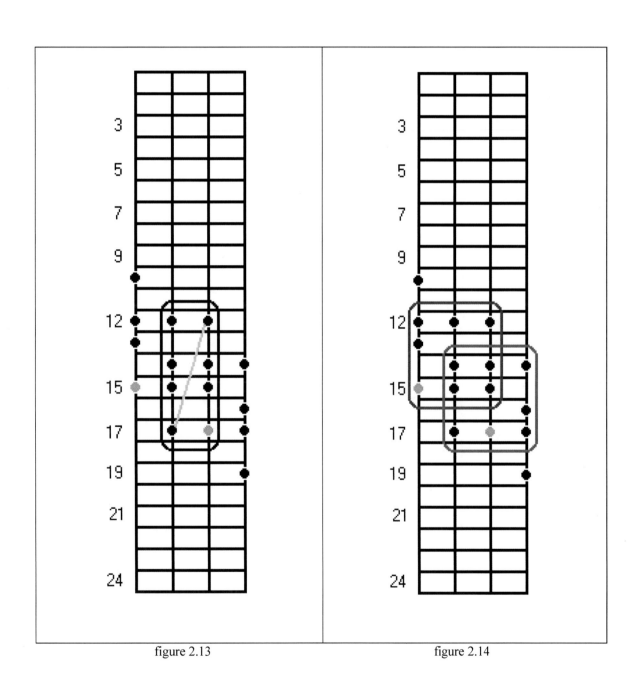

figure 2.13   figure 2.14

Box Set #2: The Locrian Mode

Figures 2.15 and 2.16 below show the placement of the roots of Locrian mode.

The Locrian roots are indicated by the yellow colored dots.

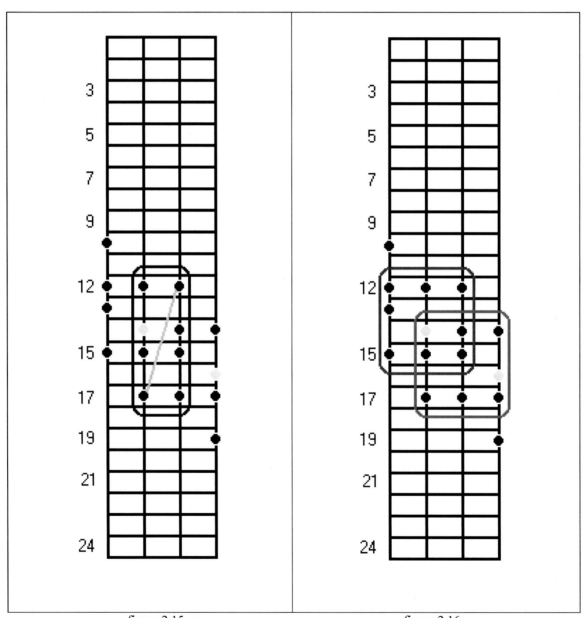

figure 2.15   figure 2.16

Box Set #2: All Mode Roots

Figures 2.17 and 2.18 below show the placement of the roots of all seven modes.

Dorian Roots = Brown
Phrygian Roots = Red
Lydian Roots = Purple
Mixolydian Roots = Orange
Aeolian Roots = Aqua
Locrian Roots = Yellow
Ionian Roots = Green

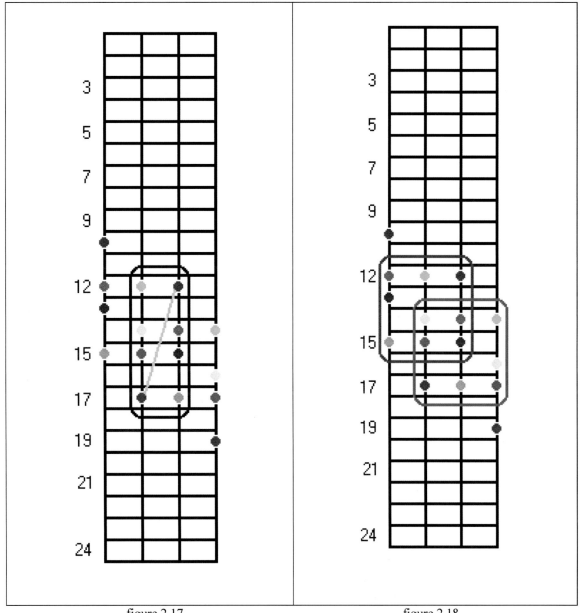

figure 2.17   figure 2.18

The same convenient feature to this system seen in "Box Set #1", is that the next note "outside the box", is always a whole step (2 frets) immediately above the highest note or likewise a whole step immediately below the lowest note.

These outside "safe notes" are represented as open circles in figure 2.19 below.

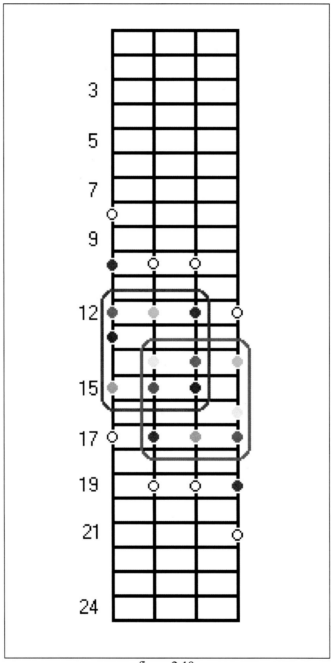

figure 2.19

**Box Set #2
with outside "safe" notes**

Combining Box Set #1 and Box Set #2

The minor tetrachords in this subsection have been color coded to aid in the recognition of the patterns and understanding of the relationships between the two different tetrachords.

The goal here is to help the bassist in visualizing the means for easily transitioning from one box set up or down to the next.

The minor tetrachord which has as its lowest note the 2nd degree of the major scale is coded brown.

The minor tetrachord which has as its lowest note the 6th degree of the major scale has been coded blue (except for the root of the Ionian/Major Scale, which provides a clear point of reference, is green).

Notice that if the minor tetrachord built off the 6th degree of the major scale (blue) is the lower of the two tetrachords on the same string, that its highest note is also the lowest note of the minor tetrachord built off the 2nd degree of the major scale (brown). The note which is shared by the 6th minor tetrachord on the bottom and the 2nd minor tetrachord on the top is "two-toned", ie blue on the top and brown on the bottom.

Also note that if the minor tetrachord built off the 2nd degree (brown) is the lower of the two tetrachords on the same string, then there is a gap of two frets before reaching the tetrachord built off the 6th degree of the major scale (blue).

These relationships hold true no matter which "Box Set" is higher or lower.

Figures 3.01 and 3.02 below combine
Box Set #1 (bottom-shaded) with Box Set #2 (top)

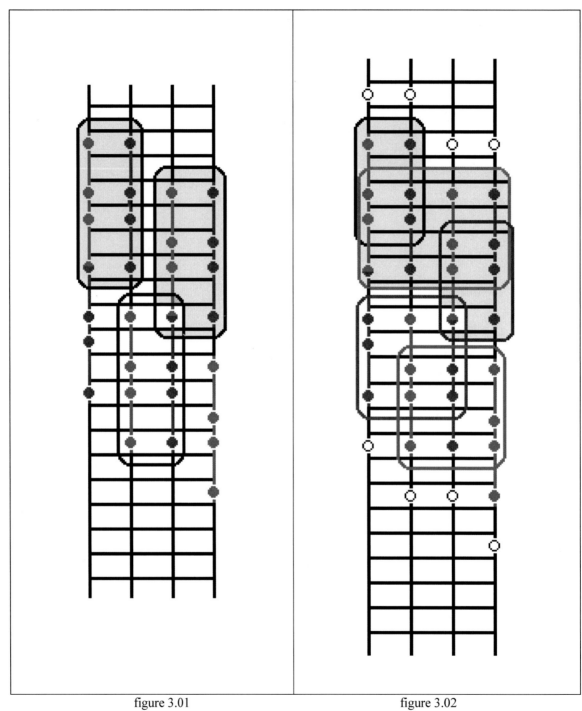

figure 3.01   figure 3.02

The following major keys are valid for the above configuration
(based on a 21-fret bass)
[The gray shaded keys indicate incomplete box sets]

Key	comments	
	Box Set #1	**Box Set #2**
Eb	no low 'safe' notes no black box no red box low purple box note = 2-0 low major root = 2-1 high purple box note = 1-3	low brown box note = 4-3 low major root = 3-6 high major root = 1-8 high green box note = 1-8
E	no low 'safe' notes no black box no red box low purple box note = 2-1 low major root = 4-0 high major root = 2-2 high purple box note = 1-4	low brown box note = 4-4 low major root = 3-7 high major root = 1-9 high green box note = 1-9
F	no low 'safe' notes no black box low red box note = 4-0 low major root = 4-1 high major root = 2-3 high purple box note = 1-5	low brown box note = 4-5 low major root = 3-8 high major root = 1-10 high green box note = 1-10
F#	no low 'safe' notes no black box low red box note = 4-1 low major root = 4-2 high major root = 2-4 high purple box note = 1-6	low brown box note = 4-6 low major root = 3-9 high major root = 1-11 high green box note = 1-11
G	no low 'safe' notes low black box note = 4-0 low major root = 4-3 high major root = 2-5 high purple box note = 1-7	low brown box note = 4-7 low major root = 3-10 high major root = 1-12 high green box note = 1-12
Ab	no low 'safe' notes low black box note = 4-1 low major root = 4-4 high major root = 2-6 high purple box note = 1-8	low brown box note = 4-8 low major root = 3-11 high major root = 1-13 high green box note = 1-13

Key	comments	
	Box Set #1	Box Set #2
A	Low 'safe' notes = 4-0, 3-0 Low black box note = 4-2 low major root = 4-5 high major root = 2-7 high blue box note = 1-9	low brown box note = 4-9 low major root = 3-12 high major root = 1-14 high green box note = 1-14
B♭	Low black box note = 4-3 low major root = 4-6 high major root = 2-8 high purple box note = 1-10	low brown box note = 4-10 low major root = 3-13 high major root = 1-15 high green box note = 1-15
B	low black box note = 4-4 low major root = 4-7 high major root = 2-9 high purple box note = 1-11	low brown box note = 4-11 low major root = 3-14 high major root = 1-16 high green box note = 1-16
C	low black box note = 4-5 low major root = 4-8 high major root = 2-10 high purple box note = 1-12	low brown box note = 4-12 low major root = 3-15 high major root = 1-17 high green box note = 1-17
D♭	low black box note = 4-6 low major root = 4-9 high major root = 2-11 high blue box note = 1-13	low brown box note = 4-13 low major root = 3-16 high major root = 1-18 high green box note = 1-18 no high 'safe' note
D	low black box note = 4-7 low major root = 4-10 high major root = 2-12 high blue box note = 1-14	low brown box note = 4-14 low major root = 3-17 high major root = 1-19 high green box note = 1-19 no high 'safe' note
E♭	low black box note = 4-8 low major root = 4-11 high major root = 2-13 high blue box note = 1-15	low brown box note = 4-15 low major root = 3-18 high major root = 1-20 high green box note = 1-20 no high 'orphan' note no high 'safe' note
E	low black box note = 4-9 low major root = 4-12 high major root = 2-14 high blue box note = 1-16	low brown box note = 4-16 low major root = 3-19 high major root = 1-21 high green box note = 1-21 no high 'orphan' note no high 'safe' note

With a 22-fret bass, add the key of "F".
With a 24-fret bass, add the keys of "F", "G" and "G#".

Figures 4.01 and 4.02 below combine
Box Set #2 (bottom) with Box Set #1 (top - shaded)

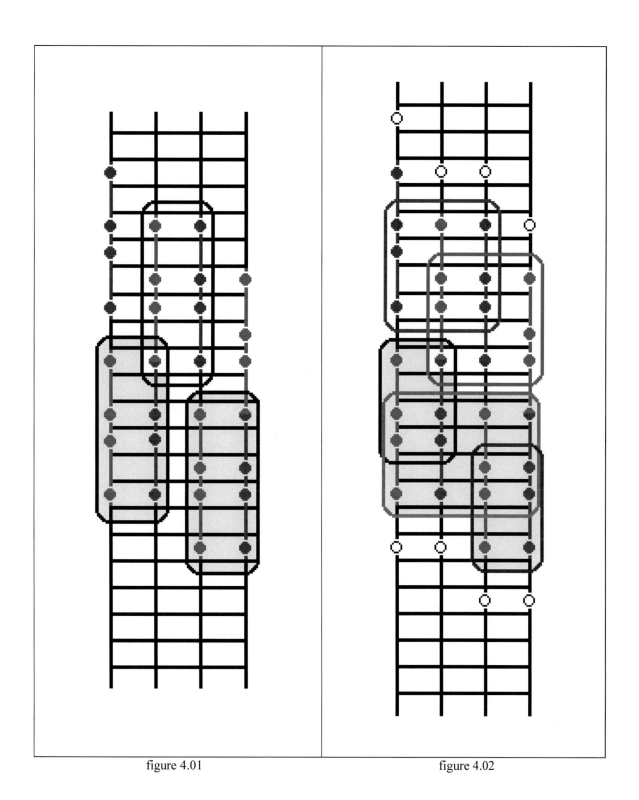

figure 4.01   figure 4.02

The following major keys are valid for the above configuration
(based on a 21-fret bass)
[The gray shaded keys indicate incomplete box sets]

Key	comments	
	Box Set #2	Box Set #1
B♭	no low 'safe' note no low 'orphan' note no brown box low green box note = 3-0 low major root = 3-1 high major root = 1-3 high green box note = 1-3	low black box note = 4-3 low major root = 4-6 high major root = 2-8 high purple box note = 1-10
B	no low 'safe' note no low 'orphan' note no brown box low green box note = 3-1 low major root = 3-2 high major root = 1-4 high green box note = 1-4	low black box note = 4-4 low major root = 4-7 high major root = 2-9 high purple box note = 1-11
C	no low 'safe' note no low 'orphan' note low brown box note = 4-0 low major root = 3-3 high major root = 1-5 high green box note = 1-5	low black box note = 4-5 low major root = 4-8 high major root = 2-10 high purple box note = 1-12
D♭	no low 'safe' note no low 'orphan' note low brown box note = 4-1 low major root = 3-4 high major root = 1-6 high green box note = 1-6	low black box note = 4-6 low major root = 4-9 high major root = 2-11 high purple box note = 1-13
D	no low 'safe' note low 'orphan' note = 4-0 low brown box note = 4-2 low major root = 3-5 high major root = 1-7 high green box note = 1-7	low black box note = 4-7 low major root = 4-10 high major root = 2-12 high purple box note = 1-14
E♭	no low 'safe' note low brown box note = 4-3 low major root = 3-6 high major root = 1-8 high green box note = 1-8	low black box note = 4-8 low major root = 4-11 high major root = 2-13 high purple box note = 1-15

Key	comments	
	Box Set #2	**Box Set #1**
E	low 'safe' note = 4-0 low brown box note = 4-4 low major root = 3-7 high major root = 1-9 high green box note = 1-9	low black box note = 4-9 low major root = 4-12 high major root = 2-14 high purple box note = 1-16
F	low brown box note = 4-5 low major root = 3-8 high major root = 1-10 high green box note = 1-10	low black box note = 4-10 low major root = 4-13 high major root = 2-15 high purple box note = 1-17
F#	low brown box note = 4-6 low major root = 3-9 high major root = 1-11 high green box note = 1-11	low black box note = 4-11 low major root = 4-14 high major root = 2-16 high purple box note = 1-18
G	low brown box note = 4-7 low major root = 3-10 high major root = 1-12 high green box note = 1-12	low black box note = 4-12 low major root = 4-15 high major root = 2-17 high purple box note = 1-19
A♭	low brown box note = 4-8 low major root = 3-11 high major root = 1-13 high green box note = 1-13	low black box note = 4-13 low major root = 4-16 high major root = 2-18 high purple box note = 1-20 no high 'safe' notes
A	low brown box note = 4-9 low major root = 3-12 high major root = 1-14 high green box note = 1-14	low black box note = 4-14 low major root = 4-17 high major root = 2-19 high purple box note = 1-21 no high 'safe' notes

With a 22-fret bass, add the key of "B♭".

With a 24-fret bass, add the keys of "B♭", "B" and "C".

Summary:

Box Set #1 consists of three boxes: One principal box (represented by the red box), and two smaller extension boxes (represented by the black box below and the purple box above).

Box Set #2 consists of two boxes: One box covering the bottom three strings (represented by the brown box below), and one box spanning the top three strings (represented by the green box above).

Notes on the "9-Box" Sets:
harmonic minor, jazz minor and Harmonic Major

In each of the "9-Box" fingering systems, all seven notes of the scale are contained on two strings – with 4 notes on one string and 3 notes on the other.

In the case of the 4-note string, one position is constant in every case:

The diminished tetrachord (constant)

R ♭2 ♭3 ♭4 / 0 1 3 4

On the 3-note string, the red diamonds below (fifth degree of both the jazz and harmonic minors; and root of the Harmonic Major) are also constant throughout. These 5 constant notes make for only 2 variables between the three scales.

Relative to the jazz minor, the variables are the 6th (in the case of the harmonic minor) and the 4th (in the case of the Harmonic Major).

The 1-string 3-note patterns (diamonds constant)

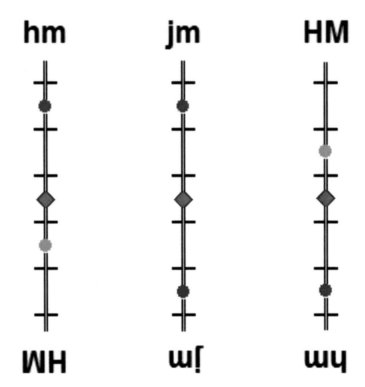

The 2-string 7-note patterns

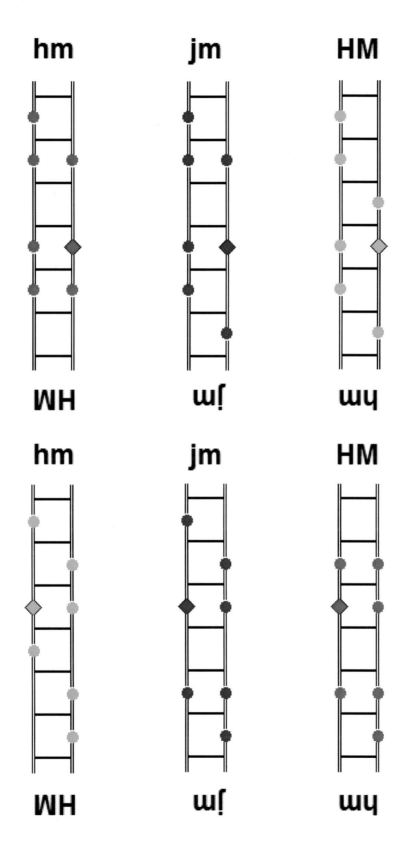

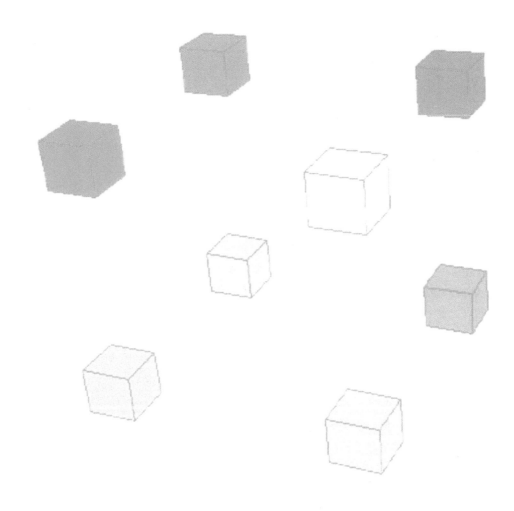

harmonic minor: 5-box set

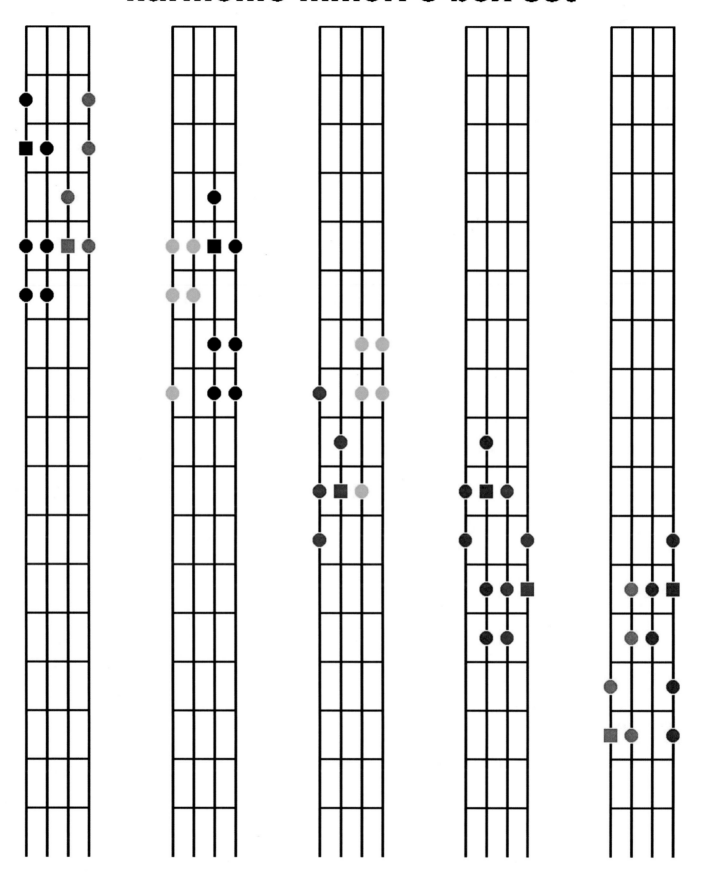

harmonic minor: 9-box set 1.1

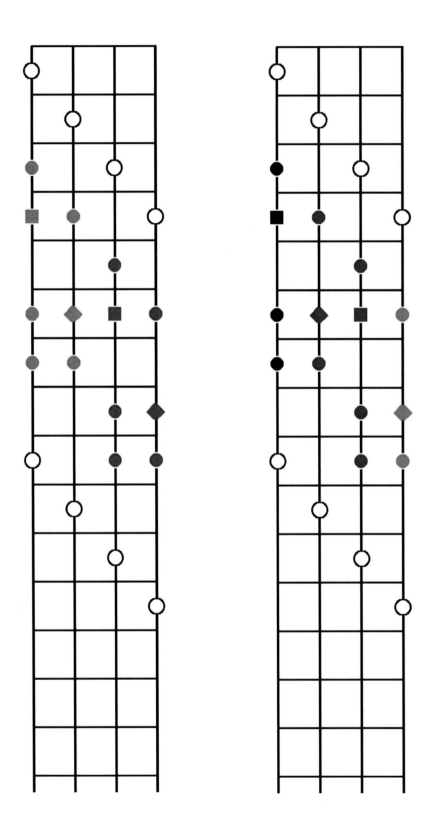

harmonic minor: 9-box set 1.2

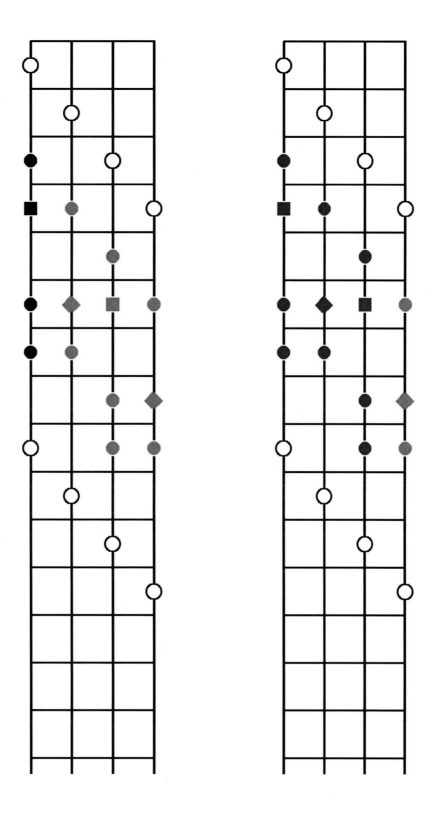

harmonic minor: 9-box set 2.1

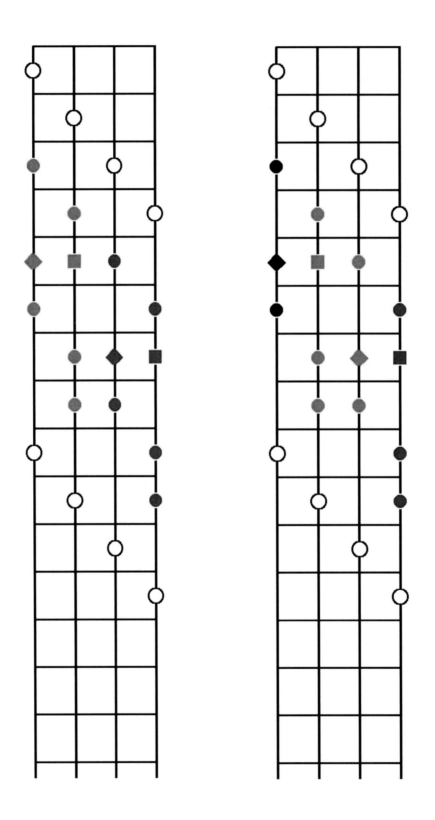

harmonic minor: 9-box set 2.2

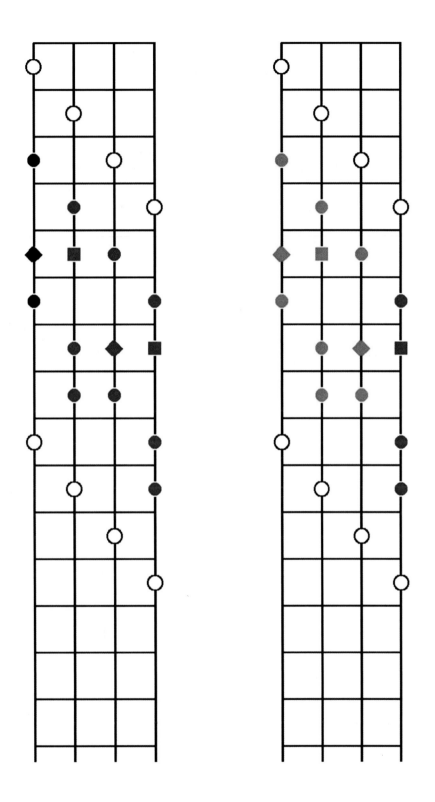

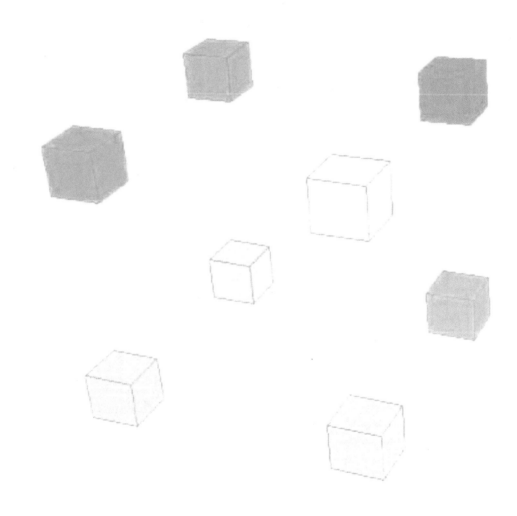

jazz minor: 5-box set

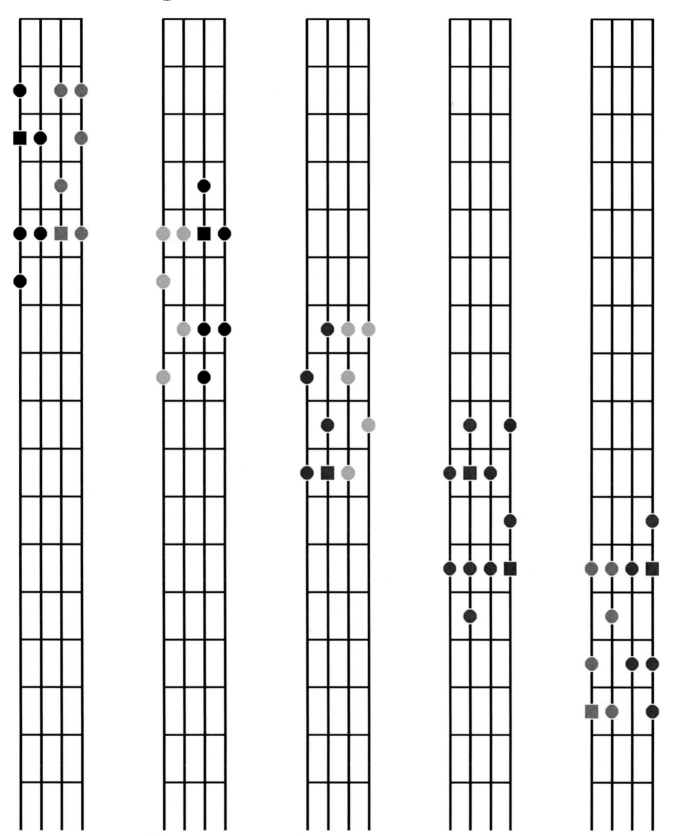

Note the mirrors between the black/purple, blue/green and red/red 2-string sets.

47

jazz minor: 9-box set 1.1

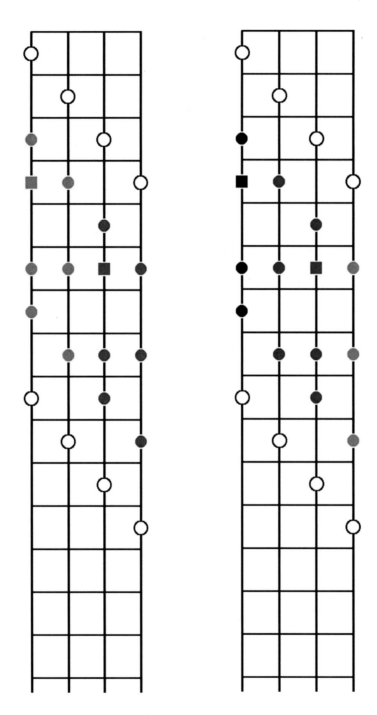

Due to the unique radial symmetry of the jazz minor (aka "ascending melodic minor"), a convenient feature to this 9-Box system here (as echoed in the 7-Box Sets qv. pages 22 and 32) is that the next note "outside the box", is always a whole step (2 frets) immediately above the highest note or likewise a whole step immediately below the lowest note. These outside "safe notes" are represented as open circles.

jazz minor: 9-box set 1.2

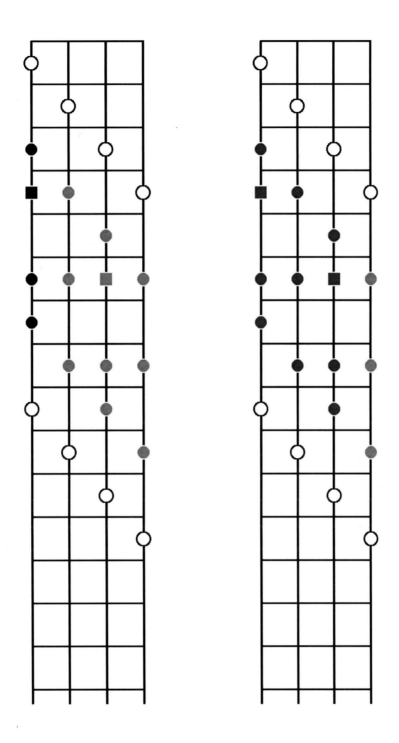

jazz minor: 9-box set 2.1

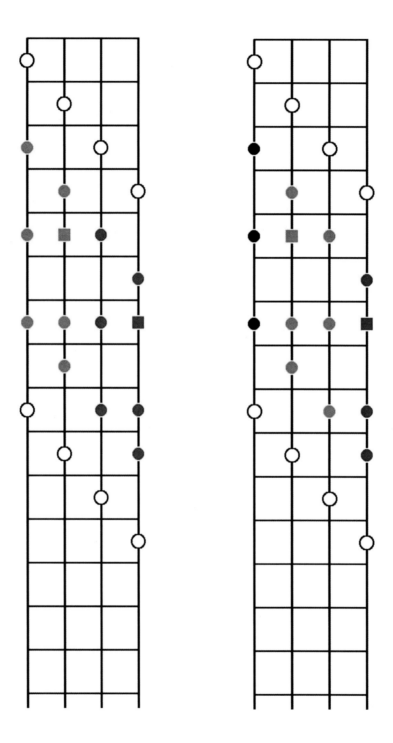

jazz minor: 9-box set 2.2

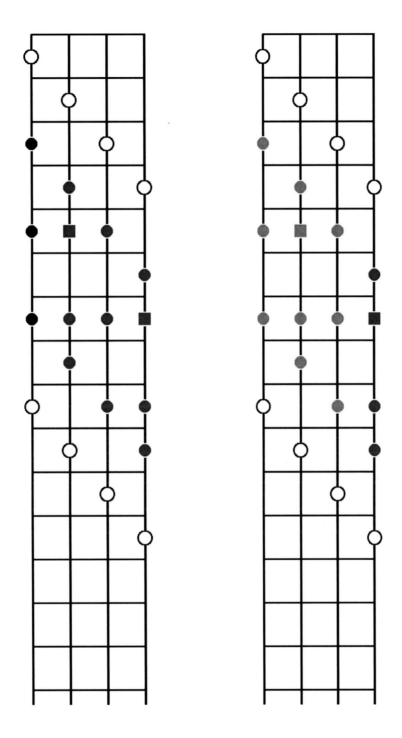

51

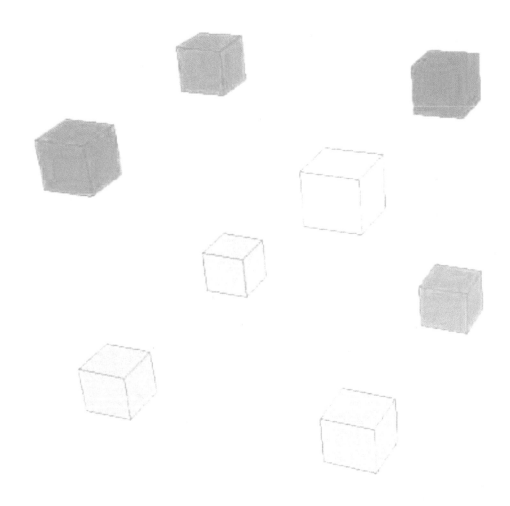

Harmonic Major: 5-box set

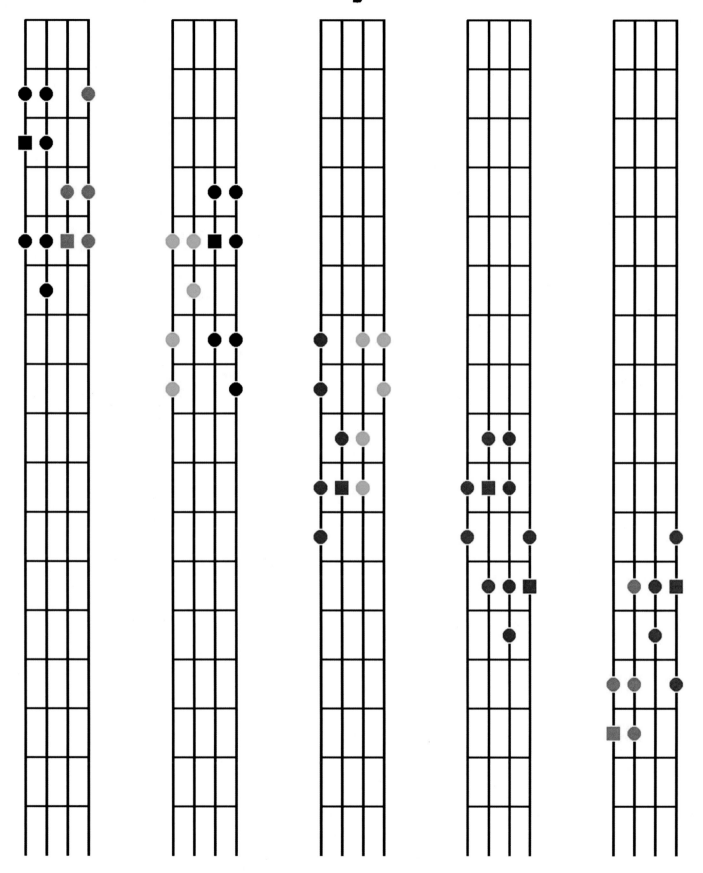

Harmonic Major: 9-box set 1.1

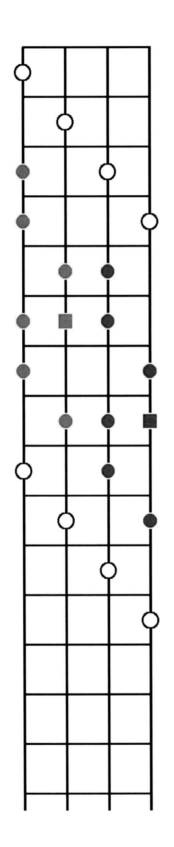
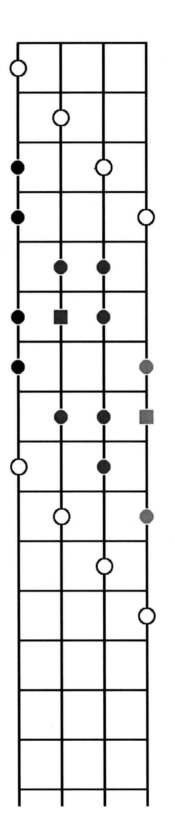

Harmonic Major: 9-box set 1.2

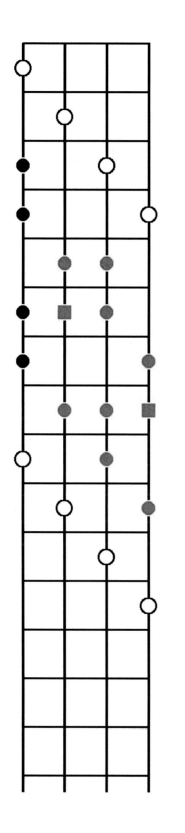
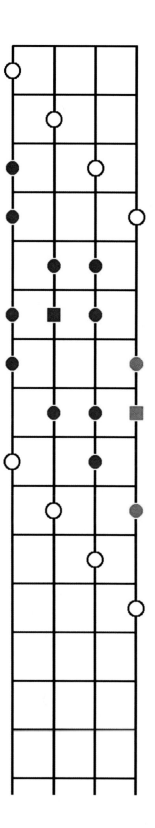

Harmonic Major: 9-box set 2.1

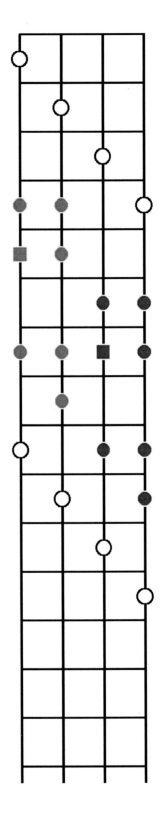
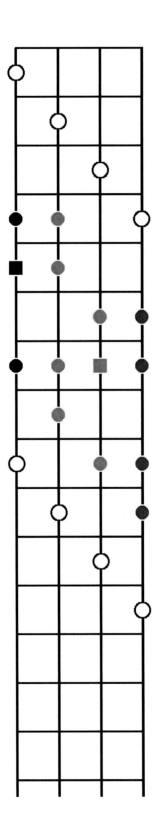

Harmonic Major: 9-box set 2.2

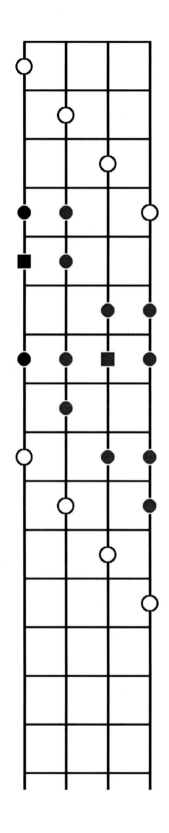
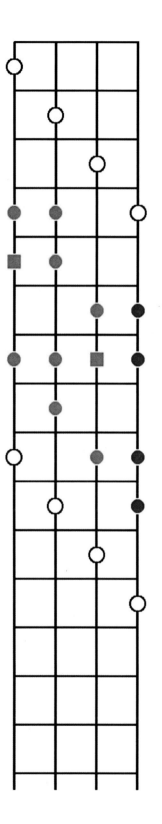

The Chromatic Cube

The "Chromatic Cube" is a graphic representation of the interlocking nature of the scales commonly used in occidental composition and improvisation.

In this standard form, the most basic scale, the diatonic major, is shown as the all-white grid facing you.

All of the arrows originate from this white corner and point towards increasingly altered scales related to this most basic scale. Following the arrows away from this "origin," the scales are enhanced in a progressive manner.

For those unfamiliar with the concept, it can most easily be understood in terms of:

1) major scales
2) melodic minor scales
3) diminished scales
4) wholetone scale
5) bebop major scale

White (shown opposite as the originating point of all arrows) is the diatonic major scale.

Red (directly to the left of the white origin) is the ii minor (melodic, ascending form) scale (#1).

Orange (at the intersection of the red and yellow) is the wholetone scale (#1 and ♭3).

Yellow (directly below the origin) is the i minor (melodic, ascending form) scale (♭3).

Green (at the intersection of yellow and blue) is the i diminished scale (i melodic minor with split fifth, ie. ♭5 and #5).

Blue (directly northeast of the origin) represents the I bebop major scale (added #5/♭6 - superset of both the I Harmonic Major and vi harmonic minor, as well as parent to many other useful structures).

Purple (at the intersection of the red and blue) is the ii diminished scale (ii melodic minor with split fifth: ♭5 and #5).

Black (at the convergence of all three secondary colors) is the major scale whose root is a tritone (♭V) away from the white origin's major root.

Once a diatonic major scale is chosen, any of its related enhanced, embellished, or otherwise altered scales may be used to exhibit various colors (levels of tension) without completely disassociating from the sound of the original pitch set.

For example, form I at the first fret represents a G♭ major scale, which may be used over a D♭7 chord (pg 62). Using the other scales, the D♭7#4, D♭7♭6 and D♭13♭9 sounds may be explored, among other even more unusual ones.

The Chromatic Cube for Bass

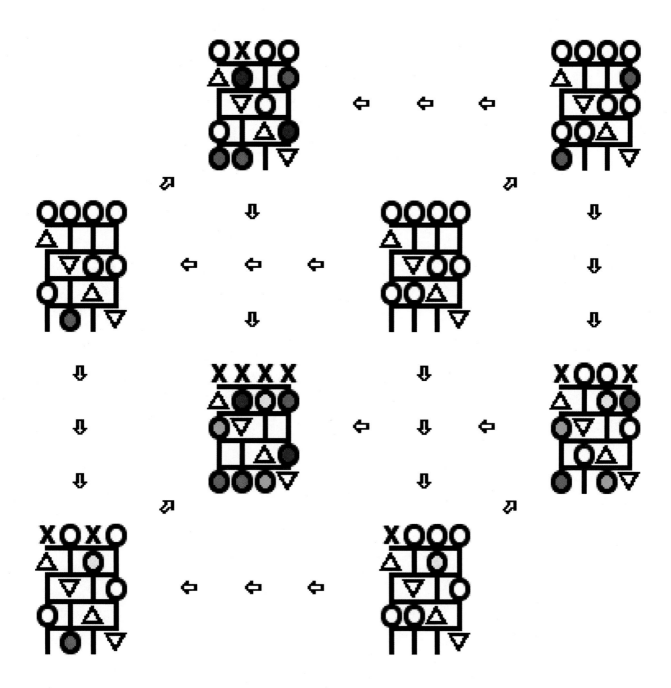

Single String Study

Choosing the primary axis to be centered at D, the secondary axis is G#/Ab.

Red is the raised root of the C Ionian parent (creating the ii jm). Yellow is the ♭3 (i jm). The Wholetone scale is a combination of the Red and the Yellow alterations (#1+♭3).

Blue is the secondary axis (I Bebop Major). Green (Blue + Yellow) and Purple (Blue + Red) are both diminished scales, and the scale at the bottom of this chart ("Black") created by combining all enhancements is the major scale whose root is a tritone away from the C Ionian parent's root (F#/G♭).

[Note that the tritone components B and F are constant throughout.]

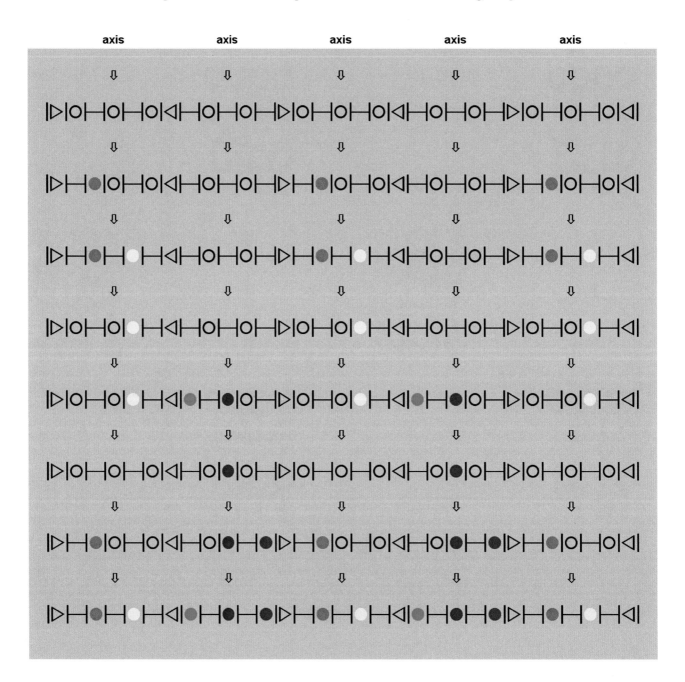

60

Study In Two Strings Tuned To A Fourth

FORM 1
POSITION 1

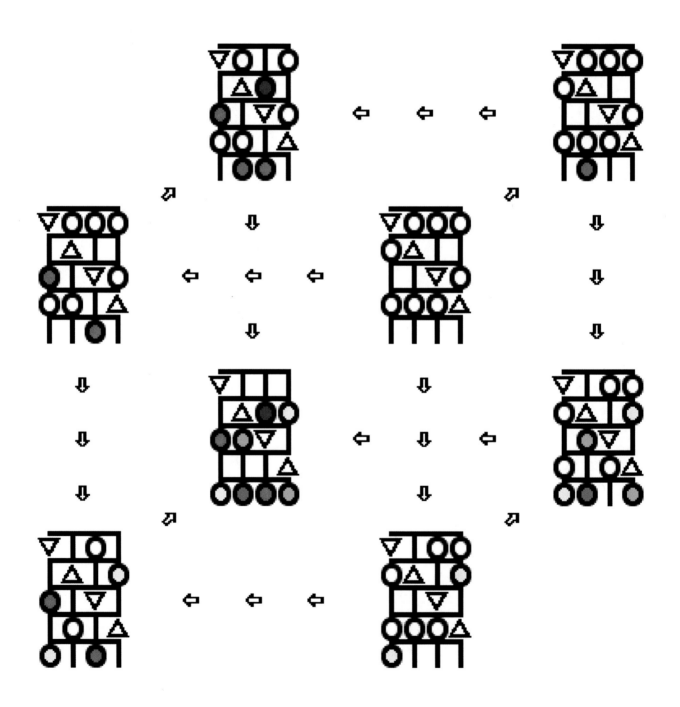

FORM 1¹/₂
POSITION ♭2

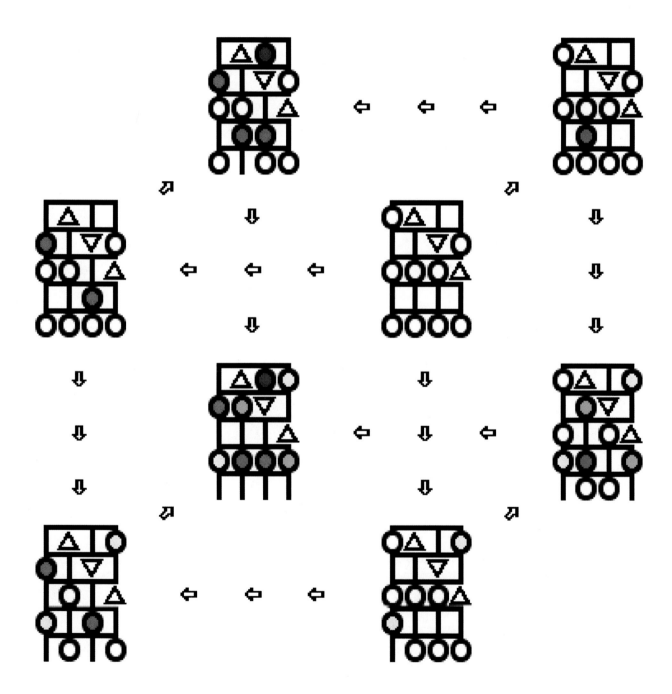

FORM 2
POSITION 2

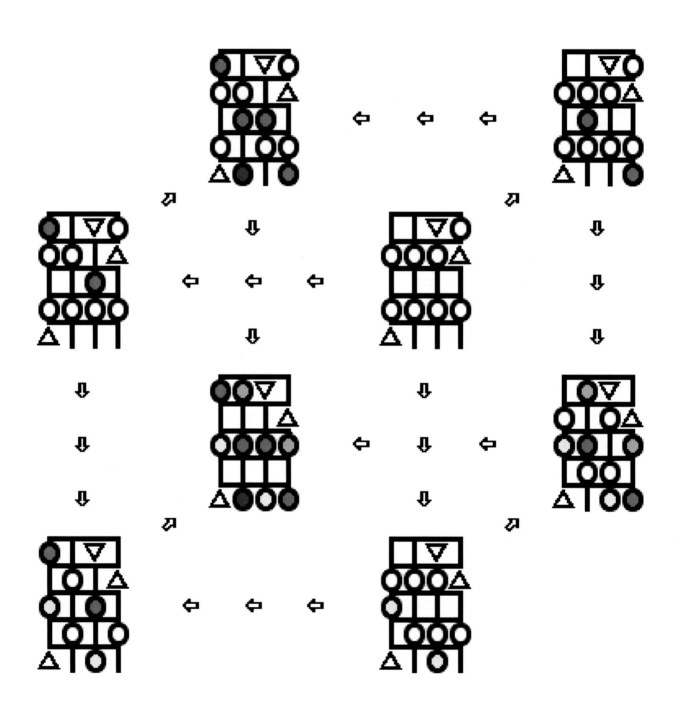

FORM 2$^1/_2$
POSITION ♭3

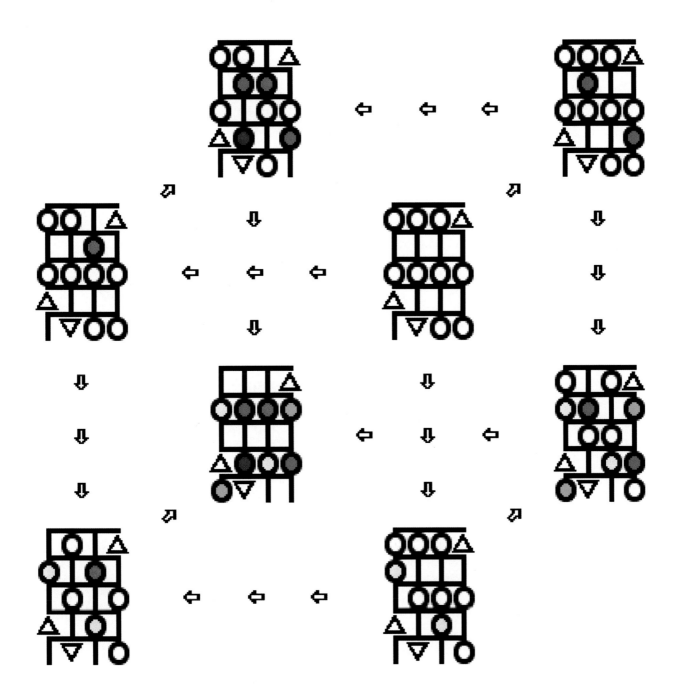

FORM 3
POSITION 3

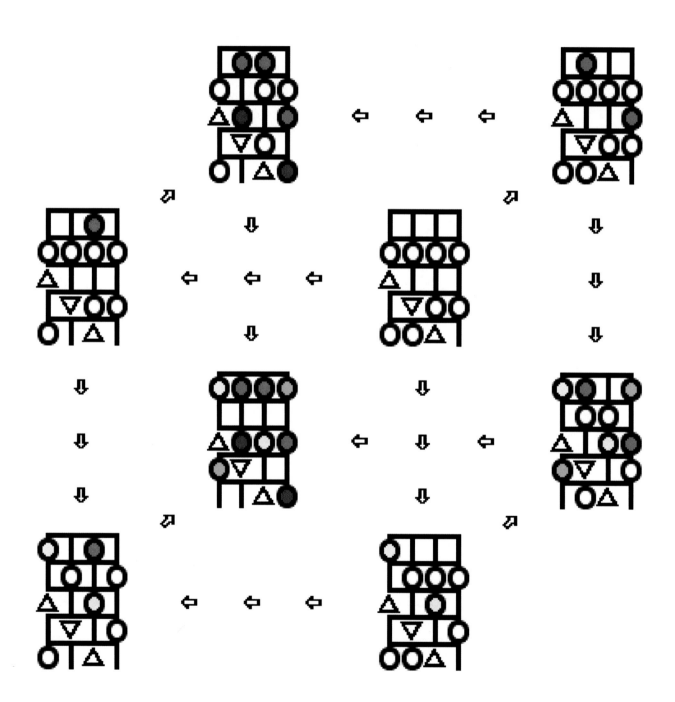

FORM $3^1/_3$
POSITION 4

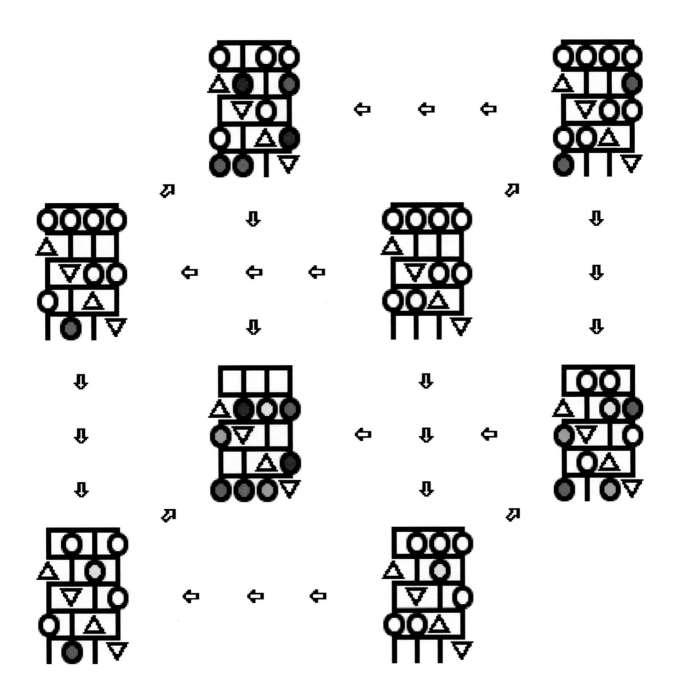

FORM $3^2/3$
POSITION ♭5

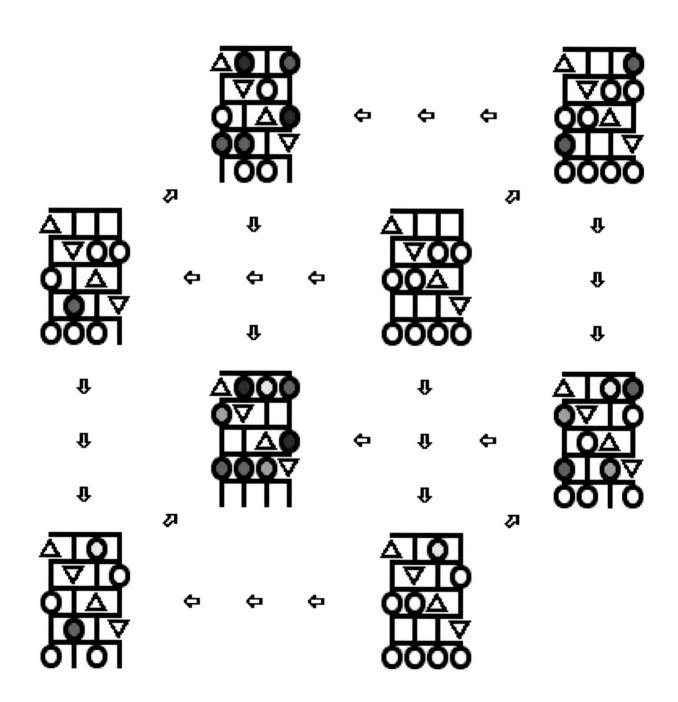

FORM 4
POSITION 5

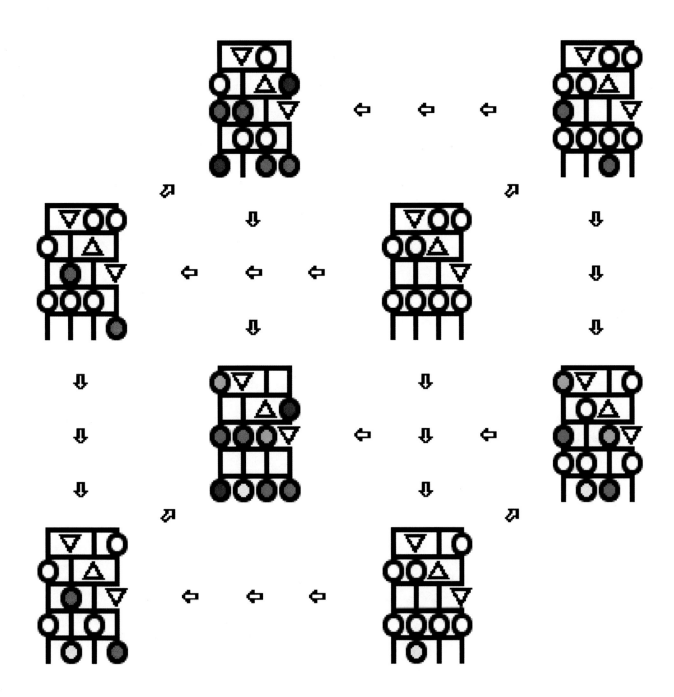

FORM 4$^1/_2$
POSITION ♭6

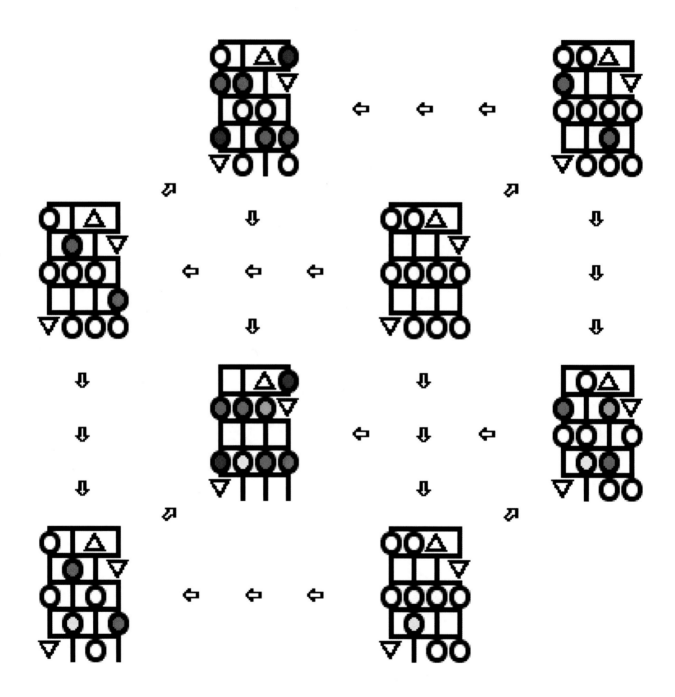

FORM 5
POSITION 6

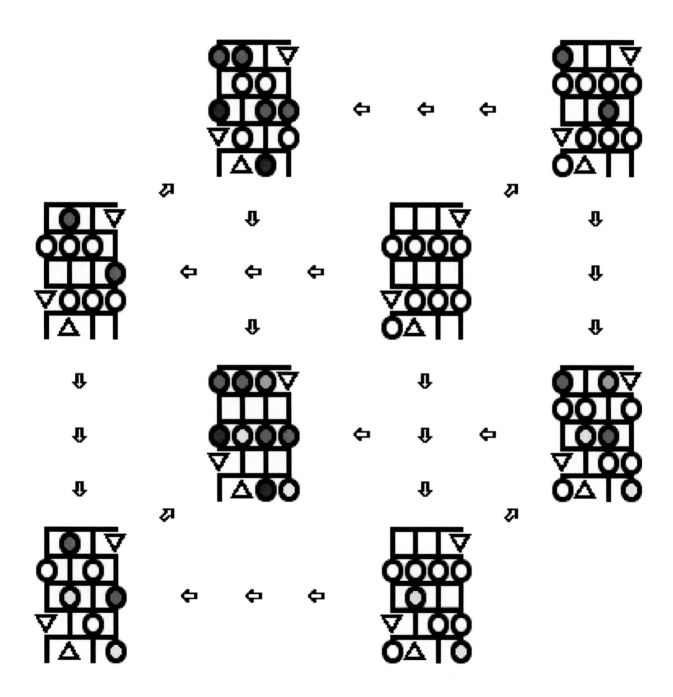

FORM $5^1/_3$
POSITION ♭7

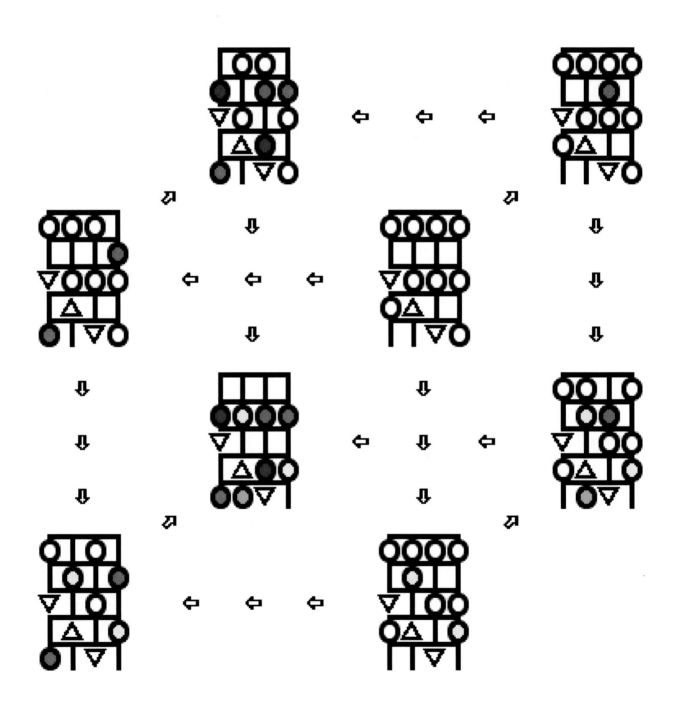

FORM $5^2/3$
POSITION 7

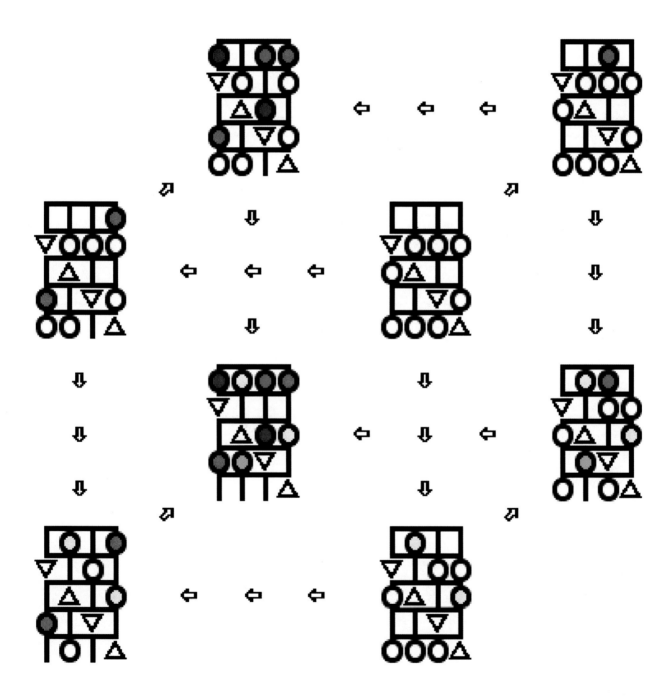

Pentatonic Scales

▲ = root of major, shown in C major

■ = root of minor, shown in A minor

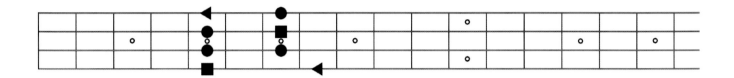

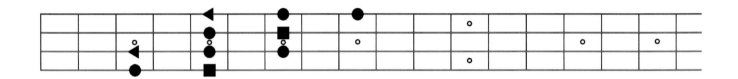

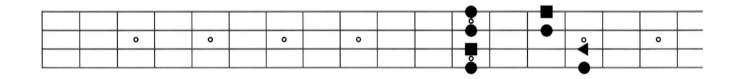

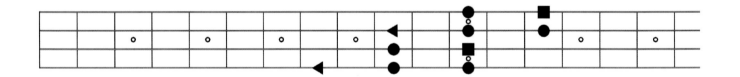

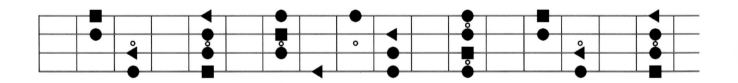

Major and Minor Pentatonic Scales

Major/Minor Pentatonics Combined:
Mixo-Dorian Bebop Scales

All modes of the octatonic Mixodorian / Bebop Dominant can be expressed as a combination of two Ionian set modes.

<u>Parent Scale: *Bebop Dominant*</u>
Bebop Dominant, Mixionian
mixolydian / ionian
major pentatonic add 4, ♭7 and 7
dominant, major

<u>2nd Mode of the Bebop Dominant Scale</u>
Doriolian
dorian / aeolian
minor pentatonic add 2, ♭6 and 6
minor

<u>3rd Mode of the Bebop Dominant Scale</u>
Phrygiolocrian
phrygian / locrian
minor pentatonic add ♭2, ♭5 and ♭6
♭2 minor with added ♭5 (altered minors)

<u>4th Mode of the Bebop Dominant Scale</u>
Lydionian
lydian / ionian
major pentatonic add 4, #4 and 7
major

<u>5th Mode of the Bebop Dominant Scale</u>
Bebop Dorian, Bebop Minor, and
"Mixodorian / Combined Major and Minor
Pentatonics" as shown in the following 3 pages
mixolydian / dorian
major pentatonic add ♭3, 4 and ♭7
minor pentatonic add 2, 3 and 6
dominant, dorian, blues

<u>6th Mode of the Bebop Dominant Scale</u>
Phrygiolian
phrygian / aeolian
minor pentatonic add ♭2, 2 and ♭6
minor

<u>♭7th Mode of the Bebop Dominant Scale</u>
Lydiocrian
lydian / locrian
major pentatonic add ♭2, #4 and 7
major

<u>7th Mode of the Bebop Dominant Scale</u>
Locrydian
locrian / lydian
half-diminished, altered 7ths

It is interesting to note that this common scale exhibits a type of dual radial symmetry:

F#		G		A		B	axis	C		D		E		F
	m2		M2		M2		m2		M2		M2		m2	

axis

C		D		E		F	axis	F#		G		A		B
	M2		M2		m2		m2		m2		M2		M2	

axis

- ■ root of major pentatonic
- ■ root of minor pentatonic
- ■ root common to both scales
- ● tone of major pentatonic
- ● tone of minor pentatonic
- ● fifth common to both scales

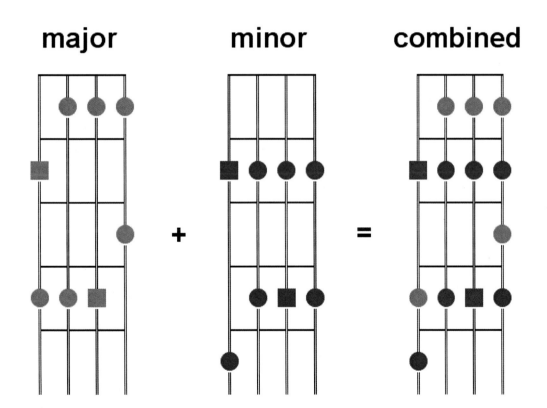

major   minor   combined

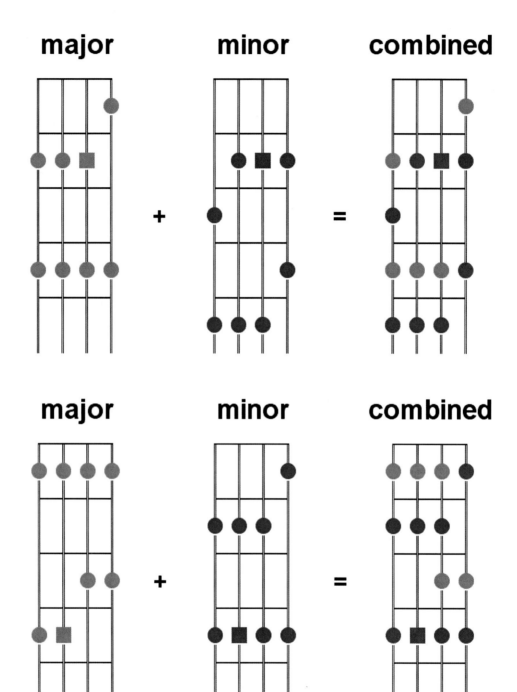

major   minor   combined

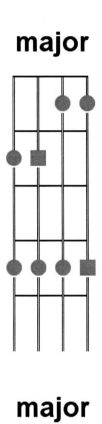 + 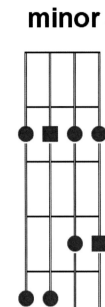 =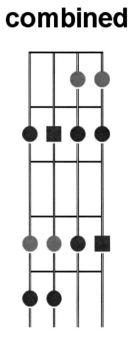

major   minor   combined

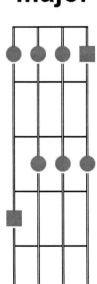 + 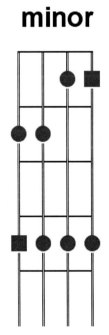 =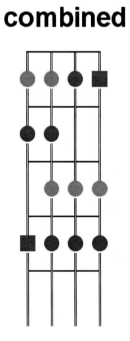

Index

About The Authors

Jeff Brent studied music theory at the University of Colorado. He is the author of the critically acclaimed music theory book ***MODALOGY – scales, modes & chords: the primordial building blocks of music*** (w/ S.Barkley). He is also a contributor to the jazz theory book ***Jazzology: The Encyclopedia of Jazz Theory for All Musicians*** (Rawlins/Bahha).

He has traveled the world as a professional musician and is the originator of the concept of Radial Symmetry in music.

Jeff lives in southern California now, gigs with his jazz combo *Trio7* and gives private lessons.

Schell Barkley is the author of of ***Fingering Mastery – scales & modes for the guitar fretboard***, (w/ J.Brent), and co-author of ***Modalogy***.

He is an accomplished musician and theorist who has authored many books on the subject of fretboard pedagogy, music theory and musicianship. Titles include his innovative ***Breaking the Sound Barrier*** guitar series and ***The Scale Book***.

Schell is the originator of the Chromatic Cube.

Acknowledgements

Bob Rawlins, Nor Eddine Bahha, Jerry Campbell, Stephen James, Bob Drewry, Adam Neely, Johnny Shines, Mark Karan, Marty David, Jean-Yves Petiot, Martin Luther, Mike Markov, Gary Paolinelli, Vic Trigger, Gene Treadway, Robert and Roland Hartley, John Greet, Tommy Galfano, Dominik Abrecht, Danu Leiser, Gil Karson, Mark Dreice, Willie Briggs, Chet Smith, Komy Ghodz, Mark Lyons, Eugene Jaceldo, Bob Dennis, Marwan Freeman, Matt Wyckoff, Phil O'Keefe, Caleb Lim, Mike Torrence, Doug McKenzie, William L. Fowler, Paris Rutherford, and Patricia Ann Phillips

visit www.FingeringMastery.com

Other Books by Jeff Brent and Schell Barkley

MODALOGY - scales, modes & chords: the primordial building blocks of music
by Jeff Brent with Schell Barkley – 2011
Primarily a music theory reference, "Modalogy" presents a unique perspective on the origins, interlocking aspects, and usage of the most common scales and modes in occidental music.

CHORDALOGY: Tonal II-V-I Progressions for the Jazz Guitarist
by Jeff Brent, Joe Bianco and Gerhard Ersdal – 2013
As a thesaurus of chordal options available to the jazz guitarist, this book is an in-depth study in fluid and cohesive voice leading using drop voicings on major and minor II-V-I progressions.

The Scale Book by Schell Barkley - 2010
The ultimate guitar scale resource book, every scale and arpeggio possible within the twelve-tone scale system is presented as standard five-fret guitar fingering diagrams.

Piano Rootless Drop-Voicing 251s by Jeff Brent - 2011
Drop-Voicings are presented to the jazz pianist within the context of both major and minor rootless 2-5-1 progressions, along with their most common altered dominants, in all twelve keys.

"Fingering Mastery" Series

Scales & Modes for the Guitar Fretboard
by Schell Barkley with Jeff Brent - 2012
The only Guitar Scale Fingering Book you'll ever need! Full-color.

Scales & Modes for the Mandolin Fretboard
by Jeff Brent and Schell Barkley - 2012
A study in fretted four-string instruments tuned to fifths. Full-color.

Scales & Modes for the Violin Fingerboard
by Jeff Brent and Schell Barkley - 2012
A study in fretless four-string instruments tuned to fifths. Full-color.

"Breaking the Sound Barrier" Series

Triads and Seventh Chords by Schell Barkley - 2009
A comprehensive review of drop-2 and drop-3 voicings for commonly used jazz chords, as well as an extensive triad study. A must-have for any serious guitarist, this book will keep your harmonies up to speed!

Chord Subs for Guitar by Schell Barkley - 2009
A detailed presentation of drop-2 and drop-3 guitar chord fingerings shown as substitutions, as well as triad subsets in a systematic and logical manner. A great follow-up for the Triads and Seventh Chords studies!

Chord Studies for Guitar by Schell Barkley - 2009
The conclusion of the "Chord Subs" series in one massive volume! Tertiary and Quartal subs for modes of the Major and Melodic Minor scales.

Scales and Numerical Theory by Schell Barkley - 2009
A fast moving guide to scale theory and improvisation for guitarists featuring song examples written by Jerry Jennings and Vic Trigger for Northern California's Guitar Activity Center. A powerful tool for visualizing the fretboard!

Chromatic Pitch Sets for Guitar by Schell Barkley - 2009
No text, no instructions, just fingerings - all of them! 4096 standard five-fret guitar fretboard diagrams show every scale and arpeggio you've ever thought of, plus all the ones you didn't - not for the timid!

Natural Harmonics for Guitar by Schell Barkley - 2010
An in-depth look at how harmonics are laid out on the fretboard which will provide the student with the means to find any harmonic on the guitar. A fabulous study for guitarists who wish to add to their musical vocabulary!

Made in the USA
Coppell, TX
07 August 2022